D0947402

To Blackie,
the first and best of my 'outside' cats.

Lessons About God I Learned From My Cat
Written by Charles Caponi
Illustrated by Tyler Hillis
Cover Design by Shawn King

Published by **Balm and Blade Publishing**
Layout and design by Matthew J. Lucio

ISBN: 978-0-9841386-8-5
Published by Balm and Blade Publishing
1927 Mountain Road
Hamburg, PA 19526
www.balmandblade.com

LESSONS ABOUT GOD I LEARNED FROM MY CAT

Charles Caponi

 # Forward

Dear Prospective Reader,

If you have opened this book far enough to be reading these words then I think I can safely draw the following conclusions about you.

First, you believe in God. Good. That's a relief. I didn't write this to try and prove beyond all doubt that God exists because I can't. I can't show you a color postcard of God's heavenly realm with a personal message to me, penned in golden ink, which says, "Having a wonderful time, wish you were here."

Neither did I write this to convince you that God is watching over us. My own personal experiences tell me that He is, but if you do not accept that testimony, I respect your position. I won't throw eggs at your house and, hopefully, you won't call me stupid (at least not until after you've read what I have to say).

So if you somehow picked the book up by mistake and are now wondering how to get out of this gracefully, the best thing to do is quietly close the book and place it back in the rack being careful not to bend the corners. And for heaven's sake don't let a hunk of gooey cheese from that slice of food-court pizza you're holding plop right into the middle of the page leaving a big greasy spot. I did that very thing at a bookstore once. I ended up having to buy the book which, when I read it, turned out to be just awful. But before you put this book back, consider for a minute that maybe you would get a kick out of the cat stories (who doesn't love a funny cat tale?). And the lessons are not burdensome (more like good common sense) so you could always give it a try (no backsies).

The second conclusion I am able to draw about you is that you're smart (this is marketing 101. Always stroke the buyer's ego). At least smart enough to realize that you're never too old to learn from your cat. After all, ancient cultures once revered and venerated the domestic cat (*felis silvestris catus*).

Cats are regal, mysterious, exotic, mystical, curious, intelligent, playful and inscrutable. Well, except the cat in this book.

My cat, Kolby (*felis fatus blobus*), is slightly obese, for the most part sedentary, and overall just your average grey Tom, who happens to be one of my best friends.

Over the three years he has allowed me to wait on him hand and foot, I've come to learn a lot about myself. While my intentions are good, as you will see, I am not always the best caregiver

Moreover, through my daily interactions with him, Kolby has shown me a lot about God, whose intentions are good and, as you will see, is always a great caregiver.

These lessons about God that I am going to share with you were all taught me to the tune of a wheezy purr and the occasional paw upside the head. I hope you enjoy them.

- Chuck

Bible versions and their abbreviations as used in this book:

American King James Version (AKJV)
Contemporary English Version (CEV)
English Standard Version (ESV)
God's Word Translation (GWT)
King James Version (KJV)
International Standard Version (ISV)
New American Standard Bible (NASB)
New English Translation (NET)
New International Version (NIV)
New Living Translation (NLT)

CONTENTS:

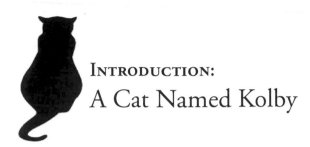

A Cat Named Kolby

My wife and I did not have children. Neither did we ever have a pet so when I decided to adopt a cat all on my own from our local Humane Society shelter; it was a big decision for me.

I was pretty much clueless in every aspect of pet ownership. That statement in itself shows you how clueless I was because, as every experienced pet owner already knows, you never really own a pet; they own you. This axiom is especially true of cats. It takes a cat about two weeks before they have the title to your property transferred into their name, and you become just a tenant graciously allowed to live under the same roof while catering to their every need.

My cat's name is Kolby, and, as I said, he is a shelter cat. He has been with me three years and is now somewhere around five years old. Of his history before he came to live with me, little is known. I do know he had a previous life with a different owner before he went to the shelter and from the shelter to me. We never speak of it.

He's a large grey-striped cat with light green eyes ringed in black. These rings give him the appearance he is wearing heavy amounts of eyeliner. To my knowledge, he is not, but then I am not with him every minute of the day and who knows what he does in private.

He is certainly not your stereotypical cat. He has no hunting tendencies (or talents) and does not display the side of a cat's nature that some find offensive such as "playing" with its' intended victim. If he finds a bug on the basement floor, he is more apt to walk on by than to stop and bat it around before eating it. Usually, he alerts me to the bug's presence with a meow and then walks off expecting me to take it from there. He reminds me very much of a small version of Ferdinand, the flower-loving bull, who would much rather smell the flowers than gore the matador. His front paws had been de-clawed before I adopted him, but he has learned to adapt quite well. He curls those paws into tiny fists and on the rare occasions he gets angry, those little fists can deliver quite a wallop as I learned one day when he punched me in the chin. But as I say, these times are rare.

He's a snuggler and a purr machine. He is always purring over something. Put out his food, he purrs. Rub his tummy, he purrs. Pull his tail, he purrs. He talks non-stop and at times I can barely get a word in edgewise. He's meowing right now (probably wants to know if I'm talking about him and am I saying only good things).

He is the pickiest of eaters. He turns up his nose at most types of canned food no matter how fancy the name sounds. Words such as "succulent," "tender" and "meaty" mean nothing to him. I can show him the statement right on the can where it guarantees he will enjoy the contents, and he still walks away unimpressed.

Mostly he likes gravy. I always buy food slathered in gravy. He laps up the gravy and leaves the meat. I don't know why cat food manufacturers don't offer gravy by itself as a menu choice. Something like "Can O' Gravy" or "Mystery Sauce" would be nice. No meat needed. I think my purchases alone would make it a profitable venture for them.

Kolby does not play. I've spent quite a lot of money on

{ Notice Kolby's strategic hiding of his gut over the armrest of the chair. This picture is from his online dating profile. }

quite a few cat toys only to give most of them away. He has little interest in toys.

In the first year of our relationship, Kolby and I had quite a few adventures as we learned to co-exist. I used those events as a basis to write a book about the adoption process and also the adaptation process. It is titled *My Adventures With Kolby, and I Don't Mean the Cheese.* It's full of funny stories and goofy happenings between Kolby and me as we learned to cohabit.

The book was then sold locally as a fundraiser for the Humane Society shelter where I first found Kolby (or, as detailed in my first book, he found me). I figured it was a way to help repay them for putting us together in the first place and for providing so many deserving animals with a second or third chance at a happy life. I would recommend it highly to anyone wishing to laugh at the antics of a self-absorbed, roly-poly male (I'm talking about the cat as I am no longer roly-poly. Self-absorbed, yes, roly-poly, no). For this book, I took another batch of our adventures and looked for the spiritual meaning that could be found in them. I did not have to look too hard. Almost daily in my interactions with Kolby

I am reminded of how God interacts with us.

In my role as caregiver to Kolby, I can see how God relates to us in His role as caregiver. I'm sure He finds us as maddening, as challenging and as endearing as I find Kolby. He laughs with us in our good times and cries with us in our times of sorrow. He shakes His head when we make yet another poor life choice and through it all He never stops loving.

For reasons that we cannot fully appreciate, we are of infinite importance to Him. This is a concept that baffles us, or at the very least it should humble us. David voices his bewilderment in Psalms 8:4 (NET) when he asks: "Of what importance is the human race, that you should notice them? Of what importance is mankind, that you should pay attention to them?" This is one of the great mysteries of God. He had every right to wipe the slate clean and start over, but He chose not to do so. Instead, on our behalf, He gave the best gift heaven had to give. He gave His Son. Unlike a magazine subscription or a Fruit-of-the-Month club membership, heaven's gift truly is the gift that keeps on giving. Happiness, wisdom, faith, strength, eternal life and so much more are given freely to those who ask. No strings attached.

And now, on to the lessons.

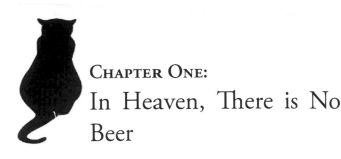

CHAPTER ONE:
In Heaven, There is No Beer

No eye has seen, no ear has heard, and no mind has imagined what God has prepared for those who love him.

- First Corinthians 2:9 (NLT)

Kolby never goes outside. Ever. That's his choice, not a decision I have forced upon him. Since he first came to keep me company, he has shown no interest in the great outdoors. I sometimes leave the front door propped open if I am carrying groceries or something large into the house and he will sit at the threshold, looking out, but he will not venture even one paw across it. It's almost as if there is an invisible force field holding him at bay.

Not that I am upset with his reluctance to go outside. It's nice not to have to fight him at the door every time I leave for work. Plus, the removal of his front claws has left him pretty much defenseless. If he did go outside he would have no natural means to defend himself and even an overly aggressive rabbit could kick his behind up and down the block. I thought about getting him a concealed carry permit but that just seemed excessive.

So I am not too concerned with his reclusiveness and his life is not a bad one, but all it consists of is bed-to-bowl-to-litter box with a very few stops now and then for some playtime. I do think that going outside under carefully controlled circumstances would be good for him. It would give him a chance to breathe in the fresh air and feel the earth underfoot and to experience all the different smells and sights and feel the unfiltered sun upon his fur. Perhaps he could eat some grass and roll in the dirt. There is so much more to this world that he will never see or experience. He needs to expand his horizons.

With this aim in mind, I thought that I would buy a harness and leash, see if I could train him to use it, and then I could walk him like a dog. We have a nice park across the street with a paved walking path that he and I could use, and the exercise would do us both a world of good.

Before you turn your face away so I can't see you snigger into your hand at the thought of a cat learning to heel on a leash like a dog, let me tell you I've already seen it done.

I was sitting in the lobby of a very posh Washington DC hotel when two exquisitely groomed young men came walking across the mezzanine. One of the men was holding a leash. On the end of the leash strode a magnificent cat.

This was not your garden variety schlub cat (sorry Kolby, the truth does hurt) but one of those exotic breeds that you get in some far off land and then bring into the country after filling out enough paperwork to choke a horse.

You would never see this cat lying on its' back in a puddle of sunlight with legs all splayed out, stomach lopping off to one side. This cat would be in a French silk dressing gown eating tuna with a teaspoon and dabbing daintily at the corners of its' mouth with a monogrammed hankie.

It was a sleek, short-haired, tawny-spotted cat, taller than a house cat, with perfect posture and tail held erect at a precise ninety degree angle. Oh, it was proud of itself all right. Indeed all three of them radiated an arrogance that you could feel. I thought about approaching them and asking how they had taught their feline to tolerate the leash, but I figured that all I would get for my query would be a haughty look, and the cat would make gestures at my shoes as if it were burying something in the sand. So rather than risk rejection, I sat mute in my chair and marveled as they swept past.

However, I did buy a harness and leash for Kolby and with much pushing and prodding got him all strapped in. Then we went outside. It did not go well. As soon as I sat him down in the grass, his legs crumpled and he tipped on his side and started to cry. He lay there and cried until I took him back indoors.

Months later I tried again. I carried him outside, this time without the harness, and took him into our fenced-in side yard. This might be a safe place to let him run a bit. As soon as I sat him down in the grass he tipped over and began to cry.

"Look, here are crunchy leaves," I said.

Pitiful meowing.

"How about some nice chewy grass?" I asked.

Louder, even more pitiful meowing.

"Bug on a stick?" I proffered, holding up a stick with a bug on it.

Tortured, soul-wrenching meowing.

At this rate, the only thing I was going to accomplish was to get a nice fat ticket from the animal control officer and a rap sheet as an animal rights abuser. I knew Kolby would have no problem ratting me out to the PETA people, so we went inside and pretended like it never happened.

Oh well, I tried. I tried to get Kolby to see that the world held so much more for him than just fifteen rooms on three different levels. But he could not grasp it. He could not rise above his own narrow conception of what his world was and what his life should be. Anything else is beyond his limited comprehension.

He does enjoy sitting in a window on a sunny day; the storm window up and the fresh air wafting through the screen. He watches the cars go past and the people walking by. Sometimes people will notice him in the window and shout a greeting. He has achieved a small degree of fame resulting from my first book about him and occasionally people will recognize him and call him by name. He does not respond. His house is the extent of his world. That is his choice.

In many ways, we are exactly like Kolby. This world is all we know and all we care to focus upon when God has so much more in store. He would like us to lift our thoughts to heaven and see that as beautiful as this world can be, it is nothing compared to what is waiting for those who are faithful. But it seems beyond our limited comprehension.

Man and nature have ravaged this world for many centuries yet there are spots still so stunningly beautiful they take our breath away. But to compare these to the beauty of heaven would be like comparing the Grand Canyon to the hole Kolby paws in his litter box right before he does his business.

Our Scripture verse tells us we cannot even begin to imagine what God has planned for us. While we cannot fathom all that His promise entails, the Bible gives us tantalizing glimpses of what waits. Clues are scattered throughout the Scriptures as nuggets of gold. From them, we can, to a small degree, get a glimpse of our reward.

Interestingly enough, the Bible probably spends more time telling us what heaven will not be like. In this process of elimination, we can see more clearly what remains.

"They will build houses and dwell in them; they will plant vineyards and eat their fruit." Isaiah 65:21 (NIV). Let's establish this right off the bat, heaven is not sitting on a cloud, playing a harp for all eternity. Surprisingly, if you were to ask the average person on the street what heaven is like, many of them would use the above description. In fact, the results of a pretend survey I just now made up show that way too many people think this is what the afterlife is like and, as a result, they don't want to go. And I don't blame them one bit. I cannot think of anything more boring than cloud sitting/harp playing. Not that I have anything against harp music. I like it. Just not as my only entertainment option for all eternity.

Not only would non-stop harping get old fast, but clouds are made up mostly of water vapor so by sitting on one you're going to get pruny in a hurry. If you want to experience this view of heaven, try putting about an inch of water in the bathtub. Then, wrap yourself in an old sheet and sit in the tub while teaching yourself to play the harp (if you decide to try this experiment, please email me some photos or better still post them directly to the Internet. We all need a good laugh). If the God I believe in can't think up a better reward than that I am in the wrong religion. Here are a few other experiences you will not have in heaven, and you won't miss them one bit. You will never again sit in a small, windowless sterile room, waiting for the doctor to bring you his report, only to have him enter and say, "There is nothing more we can do." You will never visit your mother in the care facility and have her stare blankly at you and ask, "Now, who are you again?" You will never attend another funeral. Doctors will have no clients. Nursing homes will have no residents. Gravediggers will need employment retraining.

Our bodies will go from corruptible to incorruptible in a flash, in the twinkling of an eye. We will no longer be in subjection to death, disease, old age or any of its attending infirmities. Halleluiah! I can throw away these glasses and finally have a use for a comb!

As far as our living environment goes, God Himself declares, "They shall not hurt nor destroy in all My holy mountain." Isaiah 11:9 (ESV). Never again will two rival gangs participate in a turf war that erupts in a carefully choreographed dance fight like in "West Side Story."

On a larger scale, never again will two rival governments participate in a turf war that erupts in a global conflict that takes the lives of millions of innocent people. There will be no conflict, no strife between nations, and no more war.

Perhaps one of the greatest perks heaven has for us is time. Time to us is a precious commodity. We have only a very limited supply. We dole it out carefully in small well-planned chunks. "I can give you 30 minutes on Tuesday."

On the day we are born, our own individual doomsday clocks start ticking. As we count up in years, our clock keeps ticking down in seconds. For some, it counts only a few strokes for others it ticks a long time, but for all of us it eventually hits zero. In heaven, this will not be an issue. There, we will view time much as Kolby does.

Usually when I leave in the morning, Kolby sees me to the door (unless he's had a late night of heavy snacking and is overly tired, in which case he stays in bed). Sometimes I forget to take something with me that I need for the day. I get to the car before I realize it and then head back to the house. There's Kolby at the door. He has no idea how long I've been gone. To him it could be five minutes or five days. He just knows that I was gone, now I'm back, so it must be time for supper. The passage of time has no impact or meaning for him. In heaven, we will no longer gauge our lives by the passage of years. We have all the time we need.

I have many and varied interests. Every day something new comes along that I find interesting. One thing I've always wanted to do is learn how to clog. I'm not talking about what I have been doing to my arteries for the last 35 years, I'm talking about the Appalachian folk dancing that has its roots in Irish step dance. I love to watch a good clogger ply their trade. Sadly, I have neither the time nor, to be brutally honest, the ability, to take up step dancing. I'm afraid my attempt at this style of dance would look more like a recovering drunk suffering the DTs while hallucinating the floor to be covered with fire ants that are crawling up his legs.

In this world, we are limited in time and talent. We are lucky if we have the time to learn one skill set and do it well let alone all the peripheral little things that look like fun.

In Heaven, we will be free to pursue our passions. Do you like art or sculpting? Would you like to create beautiful objects from precious stones and metals or craft fine items from gorgeous woods? Or bedazzle an old jean jacket for that matter. How about music? Do you play an instrument now? Would you like to learn to play one (other than the harp)? Personally, I love the guitar but who knows what kind of instruments heaven has hanging on the wall for us to use to praise the Lord? How would you like to sit in with the angelic choir and sing for a worship service attended by God's entire creation? Whoa! No pressure there.

Would you love to explore the universe without the need of telescopes or rocket ships and not be afraid that a Klingon battle cruiser is going to uncloak and put a photon torpedo up the old exhaust vent turning you into a mass of subatomic particulate? How about family? Is caring for and spending time with your family a passion of yours. Do you hate the fact the grandkids live halfway across the country, and you never get to see them as they grow so fast?

Is the animal world of interest to you? Would you like to spend several thousand years teaching your cat to walk on a leash? Wouldn't it be fantastic to know, from their perspective, what it means to swim with the whales or fly with the eagles? While the lion is busy lying down with the lamb, I want to lean back against the tummy of a big ole' fat polar bear and not have him size me up as just another appetizer prior to the main course.

Is nature one area of special interest? Would you love to delve deeply into the study of botany or biology to learn what makes a tick tick, or if a bee really does have knees and why that's supposedly such a good thing? Or would you rather just kick back and enjoy the sun on your face and the breeze at your back? Would you like to live life to the fullest and not be bound by the day to day drudgery of simply trying to survive? Never again having to worry about making a mortgage payment or missing the property taxes. Not being envious of that new car your neighbor just bought and that you can't afford because your kid needs braces.

Would you like to know God more fully? Isn't that what heaven is supposed to be all about? As God has said: "I will live with them and walk among them, and I will be their God, and they will be my people." Second Corinthians 6:16 (NIV). Would you like to walk along with Jesus and talk to Him as your personal friend? How about rubbing elbows with the biblical characters you've spent your life reading about? How would you like to speak with some of the great men and women of history? Personally, I would love to visit with Abraham Lincoln, although upon meeting him I would probably just stand there slack-jawed and staring until he rolled his eyes and walked away.

Hopefully, your passion is more than the simple wants of this life. Hopefully your passion is more than just sitting on the couch in your pajamas watching reruns of "Who Wants to be a Millionaire?"

Hopefully, your passion is that of Father Abraham of whom it was written, "Abraham was confidently looking forward to a city with eternal foundations, a city designed and built by God." Hebrews 10:11 (NLT).

As the old gospel song says, "This world is not my home, I'm just passing through." Don't be like Kolby, afraid to think outside your comfort zone. Expand your horizons. Look for and long for a "New Heaven and a New Earth wherein dwelleth righteousness." Second Peter 3:13 (KJV).

Hopefully, this will become our passion, our vision, our life. If it sounds like too much work or not enough fun, then feel free to join Kolby in the window. I'm sure he would scooch over a bit and make some room.

{ There's room for one more... }

CHAPTER TWO:

Olly Olly Oxen Free

I will search for the lost and bring back the strays.
- Ezekiel 34:16 (NIV)

I don't wish to alarm you, dear reader, and I'll say this as quietly and calmly as I am able.... YOUR HOUSE IS A DEATHTRAP!!!! Leave everything and get out while you still can! My advice is check into a motel or better still just pitch a tent with no running water or electricity. Have it all on one level. No stairs! Use only the heat generated by your own body for warmth. No cooking! Fire bad! Eat everything raw! Chew carefully, please!

Sorry about that overwrought outburst. I have just been reading the statistics on accidents in the home, and they are quite disconcerting.

Every year, twenty million people visit the hospital with injuries received while in the "safety" of their own home. These range from falls to fires to accidental electrocution.

I especially don't like the sound of that last one. I was jolted once when I reached into an electrical box which I assumed (wrongly) had been disconnected. As the old song goes, "zing went the strings of my heart."

I've never understood how electricity works anyway and, therefore, do not trust it one bit. As far as I can figure out, when you plug in a radio, millions of tiny little particles shuffle their feet on a piece of shag carpet while holding hands. They then touch your radio, and the resultant shock makes it possible to listen to the ball game. I don't know if this explanation passes the scientific smell test, but it sounds as good as any I have heard.

All I know for sure about electricity are the things I learned in Cub Scouts: you don't put a fork in the outlet; you don't try to toast bread while sitting in the bathtub, and you never chew on the electrical cord. This last piece of advice I have been trying to impress upon Kolby for some time now without much success.

On the headboard of my bed, I've clipped a reading light. I need to read at night in order to get to sleep otherwise my mind just continues to replay the day's events over and over like a bad You-tube clip. Then it moves on to tomorrow and even though none of it has happened yet, it makes up situations and replays those phantom events too. Stupid brain.

The cord for the light runs down behind the headboard to an extension cord which runs to the outlet. Apparently this extension cord is made of catnip-infused plastic. That is the only explanation I can come up with for Kolby's fascination with it. I certainly did not go to the pet store and ask the clerk to recommend an extension cord that was irresistible to cats.

So, Kolby likes to go under the bed and bat around the cord. I've talked to him about the dangers that this behavior presents – he is literally playing with fire – but like most teenagers, he thinks he's immortal and just doesn't care. Since he knows that under the bed is off limits, he is very sneaky about it. I'll be lying there reading and the first I know he's under there is when I hear him batting around the cord.

Tapa-tapa-tapa.

"Kolby, are you under the bed again?"

Silence for a minute.

Tapa-tapa-tapa.

"I told you NOT to go under the bed!"

"Mrrr-up?"

"GETOUTTATHERENOW!"

Silence.

"I said OUT!"

Tapa-tapa-tapa.

It's not like he has no other beds to play under. He has several choices. But this one has the forbidden fruit that he finds impossible to resist (sound familiar? Much the same as a story about a girl in a garden and a snake in a tree).

He is drawn to this cord as a moth to a flame and if you have ever seen a moth contact a bug zapper you know why I am concerned. I guess I've seen National Lampoon's "Christmas Vacation" too many times, and I keep thinking of the scene where the cat chews through the electrical cord. I don't want that to happen to Kolby.

One night, it's very late, and I can't sleep. It's around midnight, and I am still reading. Just as I get ready to turn out the light and drift off, from under the bed I hear:

Tapa-tapa-tapa.

"Kolby, out now!"

Tapa-tapa-tapa.

"C'mon, I was almost asleep and I have to work tomorrow."

Tapa-tapa-tapa.

"All right, that's it! I'll drag you outta there by your tail if I have to!"

Silence.

Flipping the covers on the floor, I got up and knelt by the bed. I'm like a lot of people who use the space under the bed for extra storage. Under this one, I have a guitar and several boxes

of photos and such. I can't see him so he must be hiding behind the guitar case. I pull the case out and catch a glimpse of him scooting between two boxes. He's far enough back that I can't reach him. I reach in and pull out the box he's hiding behind. He moves to the far side of the bed. I jump over the bed and make a grab for him. He nimbly sidesteps my grasp and goes back to the side I just left.

No way am I playing cat and mouse (or cat and human) for the next hour. The only way to get to him is to expose him so I grab the headboard and with a mighty shove from my rippling muscles, push the bed out from the wall. There he squats like a giant furry toad, a look of total surprise on his face. Before I can get my hands on him, he runs.

Well, at least he's out from under the bed now. But look at that mess! There are dust balls under there the size of a baby's head not to mention enough loose fur to make at least two more cats. I can't just shove the bed back and go to sleep on top of this pile of dirt, can I? Can I? No? All right, I'll clean it up.

By now it's almost 1AM, and here I am on my way to the kitchen closet for a dust mop and a can of Lemon Pledge (it's not really Pledge, it's a no-name knock-off called "Fruit Scented Dusting Spray" or some such thing).

Back in the bedroom, I sweep the floor and dust all the boxes and the guitar case while Kolby watches from the hall wondering why I am not asleep yet because now he's tired and ready for bed. It's always about him.

Sliding the bed back to its original position, I smooth out the blankets and sheets and climb back in. Ah! That's the ticket. I punch the pillow into just the right shape, lay down my weary head and close my eyes.....

Tapa-tapa-tapa.

Oh for cryin' in the soup! I reached out, grabbed the extension cord, yanked the plug from the socket and went to sleep.

The question here is why I would go through all this rigmarole so late at night? The answer is simple. I love Kolby, and I don't want anything to happen to him. Oh sure, he drives me nuts every once in a while but I would do most anything to make sure he is safe. If he got hurt, it would hurt me, as well. I'll figure out a way to get that cord out of his reach and I won't have to worry about it anymore.

There is a parable in the Bible that illustrates God's love for us and to what ends He will go in seeking us out and bringing us to safety. It is the story of the Good Shepherd and the one lost sheep.

The occupation of a shepherd was not exactly one of your Fortune 500 executive positions. No one graduated from Hebrew U with a Masters in sheep management, yet at a time when nearly all of your wealth could be tied up in sheep, having a good shepherd was imperative to your financial success. It was a job that carried great responsibility. It also taught some very important life lessons.

Some of the greatest Biblical personages were shepherds

at some time in their lives. Moses (AKA Charlton Heston) was a shepherd for forty years before he graduated from leading sheep to and from their pastures to leading the Israelites from Egypt to the promised land. David spent his tweens as a shepherd and twice risked his life for his flock. It was a motley bunch of shepherds who were chosen that Holy Night to hear the announcement, and spread the news, that the Messiah had been born.

"All of us like sheep have gone astray; each of us has turned to his own way." Isaiah 53:6 (NAS). There's the problem. Without the Shepherd's leading, we tend to wander off on our own.

Does it bother you to be compared to a sheep? Well, it shouldn't as we share much in common. Contrary to what we might think by looking at them, sheep are pretty smart. Test results show that they score only slightly lower than pigs on their SATs making them ideal candidates for any upper-level community college.

Sheep are gregarious in nature and love a good party as long as there is dip (Get it? Sheep dip. I made a funny). While sheep are social creatures who enjoy the company of one another, they like a clearly defined "safety zone" of personal space too. They will follow a strong leader and usually when one sheep moves, they all do. They have a flight mentality and will run when afraid (just like me).

So Jesus told the story of the shepherd who discovered that, of the one hundred sheep in his charge, one was missing. Rather than just shrug and say, "Well, at least I have ninety-nine left." The shepherd sees to the safety of his flock and then goes in search of the missing one. No matter that it may be a fruitless task. The sheep may have fallen in a ditch or off an embankment. It may have been taken by a lion or bear. The shepherd will search until he finds the animal. When he does find it, happy as a clam, he carries it home. He does not drag it home by the tail (like I would have done to Kolby that night). He carries it on his shoulders to safety. When he is back, he does not disparage the sheep to his friends, "What a stupid sheep! It doesn't even have enough sense to stay with the rest of the flock!" Instead, He calls upon his friends to rejoice with him. He has found that which is important to him.

We are important to God. Or should I make it more personal and say that you are important to God? It took only one sheep to get the shepherd out searching. Let me put it this way, If all of the rest of us were very, very good, and you alone were very, very bad, still Jesus would have gone through everything He did. He would have left heaven just for you. He would have walked this earth with no place to lay His head just for you. He would have been beaten just for you. He would have been mocked just for you. He would have been tortured just for you. He would have died just for you.

So what are you going to do about it? Let me include myself in that question. What are we going to do about it?

Personally, I don't like being lost. I've gotten myself lost in the big city on more than one occasion, and it is not very much fun. Like the time a friend and I drove to Chicago to attend a Musical Instrument expo. This was long before there was such a thing as a GPS, and we were just two hicks from the sticks who managed to get themselves completely lost on a Saturday night in the wrong part of town.

Chicago at the time was in the midst of racial turmoil. There had been white supremacy marches in Skokie just the day before and two racially motivated murders in the area we were now driving through. Tempers were running hot.

Round and round we went, passing the same seedy looking shops and the same rough looking crowd over and over. The first few times were quite intimidating. By the fifth or sixth time around the same block, they began to feel more like family to me. I almost waved a friendly hello but then thought better of it. For their part, outside of a few long stares, they pretty much ignored us. Apparently we were not seen to be a threat at all. They probably had bets on how many times we'd have to go around the block before we found a way out.

Unlike the sheep (or Kolby for that matter), we know that we are lost. We know that the shepherd is searching for us. If we choose to, we can stay lost. We can play cat and mouse with Him for the rest of our lives if we wish.

Joshua put it very bluntly to the children of Israel when he said, "If it is disagreeable in your sight to serve the Lord, choose for yourselves today whom you will serve." Joshua 24:15 (NASB). I don't want to be lost anymore. I've caused the Shepherd enough grief and would just as soon stay with the flock from now on out. You may do as you choose as long as you stay out from under my bed.

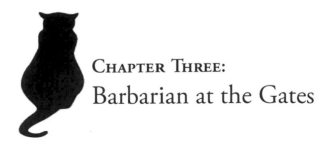

CHAPTER THREE

Barbarian at the Gates

So Peter opened his mouth and said: 'Truly I understand that God shows no partiality, but in every nation anyone who fears him and does what is right is acceptable to him.'

- Acts 10:34-35 (ESV)

I n my opinion, the position in life that brings not only the most reward but the most responsibility is that of a mother. The young minds that are trained and guided by their mothers are the same minds that grow up to be the movers and shakers that shape our world. Who knows, perhaps if little Adolph had gotten a few more swats on his rosy-cheeked bottom the world may have avoided paying a terrible price through death, devastation, and war.

Speaking of war, when our young men (and now women) march off to battle they are fighting to preserve the American way of life which, in my day, was: Mom, Apple Pie and Baseball (or hot dogs, I can never get that one straight). With the many changes in America over the past fifty years, today that list might comprise: Mom, a double half-caf Mocha Cappuccino and Xbox 360 (or hot dogs). Still, mom is at the top of the list as well she should be.

That is why I am happy to announce that I have joined that fraternal sisterhood of mothers. I am now a standard bearer in that most sacred of all vocations. I have become a mother. This is quite an achievement for a 61 year old man, and I am justly proud. In reality, I have been a mom for the past three years, but I just now found out.

Recently I was reading an article on how cats relate to human beings. This article had been written by very smart people who wear white coats plastered with pocket protectors that are stuffed with an assortment of pens. These people carry clipboards, and their jobs are to stare at things through large windows and then write down what they see. No, these are not window peepers; they are scientists (although I am sure there may be some overlap as the two occupations are not mutually exclusive).

Scientists are extremely intelligent, and it is a well known fact that they never make mistakes (*cough*, Piltdown Man) so I can assume what I read in the article is true.

The article claimed that domestic cats view humans as bigger, non-aggressive cats. In other words, cats think we are cats too. Sweet.

Moreover, the article stated, cats identify their primary human caregiver as their mother. Apparently cats don't remember much of their kitten years except the attention they received from mommy. If you are the one who puts out the food. If you are the one who brushes their fur. If you are the one who provides the lap for snuggling, you are their mother. By this reasoning then, I am Kolby's mom.

Kolby remembers nothing of his father and why should he? His father was never around. Who was it up late at night rubbing Kolby's sore tummy while his father was out catting around town?

Who was it waiting patiently with him at the vet's office while that no good Tom was chasing after the trampy Siamese who lives down the block? That's right; it was me!

I think I've done pretty well as a single mom. Kolby and I share a close relationship. We don't argue and fight. I don't need a spray bottle filled with water to discipline him as he does nothing that needs disciplining. He's a good boy that brings pride to his mother's heart. However, unbeknownst to the two of us, a storm was brewing that would soon cast a black shadow across our happy home. A shadow that would breed anger and hate. A shadow that would bring fear, revenge, and ultimately violence. Just a minute.......I had to go turn on a light. I scared myself.

It all started last year around the time of Kolby's birthday. Now, I am not one of those moms who go overboard at Christmas and birthdays. Kolby did have a party with guests invited for the first birthday he spent with me. That was a special one-time event. It is not the norm. Neither do I let his birthday pass without notice. This time I was trying to think of a nice present to get him. I wanted some form of a treat to set his birthday apart. Toys were no good as he does not play with toys. Toys require effort. That is something he avoids at all costs. Food was the most logical choice, but the problem is he is such a finicky eater it's hard to find him something he likes. I've tried so many different types and brands and have not had much success. I've narrowed it to a few taste groups that he will eat on a regular basis but finding him something new to try would be a challenge.

I went to our local pet store to check out new food options. Usually I buy whatever is in the pet aisle at the grocery store but since I wanted something unique I thought it best to try a specialty store. There were hundreds of choices. After perusing them all, I settled on a very expensive bag of gourmet dry food that promised it was everything and more that any cat could ever want or need. Only the finest ingredients had been used, and there were no fillers or other such nonsense added. At the price, it must have contained chunks of real gold too. It was $9.49 ($10 with tax) for a tiny bag that held perhaps three bowls worth of food. But it was his special day.

On the morning of Kolby's birthday, we went downstairs as usual. He sat patiently by his bowl as I got out his new treat. He watched as I filled the bowl with delicious (by that I mean expensive) food. I stood back anxious to see him dig in.

"Happy birthday!" I said.
He looked down at the food and sniffed it. He looked up at me.
"Good stuff, huh?" I encouraged him.
He sniffed it again, like someone would sniff at a dirty sock.
"Try it. Mmmm, tasty!" I said.
He sat down and stared at the bowl.
"Do you have any idea what I paid for that? EAT IT!"
He walked away.

That afternoon, the bowl remained untouched. By evening, it was clear he would not be eating this food. It was also clear I just flushed $9.49 ($10 with tax) down the proverbial toilet. Talk about casting your pearls before swine.

No doubt about it, Kolby is spoiled. I have no idea who is responsible for this. I know it is not me. I'm a good mother. I think it's probably some defect in his genes that make him this way. That's my story, and I'm sticking to it.

There was no way I was going to let this food go to waste. So Kolby didn't want it? Fine, there were others who would be happy to eat it, and they were probably right outside our kitchen door. I took the bowl of rejected food and put it outside on the kitchen steps. At this point, I didn't care who ate it. Squirrels, rabbits, Bigfoot, it made no never mind to me. Some creature, human, animal or otherworldly, was bound to eat that food.

The next day, the bowl was empty, so I put out another. This one also disappeared overnight. As I put out the third and final bowl of Kolby's rejected birthday food, I was curious about who was eating it, so I kept watch that night and sure enough around 9pm, the culprit arrived.

{ Blackie, as seen through a glass darkly. }

It was a small, jet black cat with deep emerald green eyes. The minute those eyes saw mine looking out through the kitchen window they were gone. Sometime in the night the little cat returned for, in the morning, the food was gone.

I had intended only to get rid of the unwanted birthday chow but now that I had seen the hungry little cat that was eating it, I did not have the heart to cut him off. Besides, Kolby never eats all of his wet food, and I often end up throwing some away. So I began to take what Kolby left, mix it with some dry food and put it out for the little cat I had now named Blackie.

Kolby wanted no part of my mission of mercy. He knew something was going on with his food that he did not like. He watched me carefully as I took the food he refused to eat and put it just outside the kitchen door. His keen sense of smell told him another cat had been up on the kitchen landing, and he looked at me reproachfully.

"Listen," I told him, "you were living in a shelter with lots of other cats before I adopted you. You were an outsider once too. You can put up with this cat. It won't kill you to be nice." He walked away with his tail whipping the air.

It's no hardship for me to feed another cat. I have enough money that the few extra cents it takes to fill up Blackie presents no problem with my monthly budget. Plus, as I said, what Kolby rejects, Blackie gobbles up. I'm not taking anything away from Kolby to feed Blackie. He gets his share and more. The crumbs from his table mean survival to Blackie. He may not be of my house, but there is room for him at the all-night Caponi diner.

The way Kolby views it, Blackie is an outsider. He should be sent away into the night, not rewarded with food from our table. I'm his mom. I should not give my time or attention to anyone else. I, in turn, view it as a matter of the greater good. Blackie is a homeless, hungry cat, and I'm happy to feed him for as long as he comes around. I have enough love for two.

The poor woman came to Jesus with an urgent request. "Lord, Son of David, have mercy on me! My daughter is demon-possessed and suffering terribly." Matthew 15:21 (NIV).

This woman was a Canaanite, long-time enemies of the Jewish people. The disciples wanted nothing to do with her and demanded that Jesus send her away. She was not of their house. Of all the nerve. Jesus was their messiah, not hers. On top of that, she was making such a loud noise with all her wailing they could hardly hear each other being critical of her. How rude was that?

On the surface, Jesus seemed to take their words to heart for He addressed her in a cold and condescending manner that was completely out of character for Him. He compared her to a dog that did not deserve to be fed. He told her His miracles weren't for her. She was an outsider. She was not of the chosen people. How dare she just show up and have the chutzpah to ask for His blessing? Not gonna happen.

But she was persistent. She wouldn't take no for an answer. She would endure any insult He offered. Her daughter's life was at stake. Bowing in humiliation, she said, "Even the dogs eat the crumbs that fall from their master's table." At this deep profession of faith and humility, Christ gave her the miracle she was hoping for. Her daughter was healed.

The lesson had been taught. The faith of the outsider was proven to be as genuine as the faith of those already called family. Through Christ's demonstration, the disciples saw that their narrow territorial way of viewing others was not God's way. They learned that everyone is welcome at the banquet table in God's house as long as they come in faith.

Really now, they should have already known this. These were men who studied the scriptures and Isaiah had already written, "for My house will be called a house of prayer for everyone." Isaiah 56:7 (ISV). Jesus would later quote this very verse Himself. But the disciples were too busy keeping people out of God's house to hear the message that said let them in (if there ain't a lesson in there for us Christians today, I'll eat a bowl of Kolby's leftovers).

Have you ever felt like an outsider? I know I have.

I attended a wedding once where my wife was part of the Bridal party. At the reception, while my wife was seated at the bride's table, I was seated way in the back of the hall by the door. Around the table were people who knew each other but did not know me nor I them. Not a big deal except that I am absolutely horrible at making small talk with people I don't know. I've always been this way. I would rather stand up in front of a thousand people and talk for twenty minutes on a subject I know nothing about than make a few minutes of small talk one-on-one with a stranger. For one thing, I can never think of anything to say that doesn't sound stupid to my ears, and honestly, I have a difficult time feigning interest in such shallow talk.

So, as they rambled on in conversation with one another, I

painted a smile upon my face and sat there quietly, hoping against hope that someone would pull the fire alarm. Every so often I would toss in a comment that had no bearing whatsoever on the conversation. It was awful.

Female guest number one: "What a lovely wedding."

Male guest number one: "Yes, just beautiful. I think one of the nicest I've attended."

Female guest number two, turning to address me: The bride was radiant, wasn't she?"

Me: "I like spaghetti."

Female guest number two: "How nice."

As "Lonesome" George Gobel once put it, "I feel like the whole world's a tuxedo, and I'm a pair of brown shoes." Well, in the kingdom of God there are no brown shoes.

We were all outsiders at some point in our lives until we were adopted into the family of God. Like Kolby at the shelter, we had no real place to call home. No place we belonged. No one to take us in. Until we met Jesus.

We no longer live on the cruel and dangerous streets of sin but are now joint heirs with Christ in His home. Unlike Kolby, or the disciples for that matter, we should rejoice at every brother or sister God adds to the family.

Jesus said, "I tell all of you, many will come from east and west and will feast with Abraham, Isaac, and Jacob in the kingdom from heaven." Matthew 8:11 (ISV).

In high school, it was very important to be seated at the "cool kids" table in the cafeteria. You know the table. It was populated by the Jocks and their cheerleader babes. Or maybe it was just one table with just one guy sitting at it. The leather-jacketed rebel who lived by his own rules and all the girls found so dreamy. Most often I was stuck with the nerds (or more accurately, they were stuck with me). In heaven everyone will be seated at the "cool" table (even me). Whether you come from the north, south, east or west makes no difference. If you are in

Christ, then you are an heir to a wonderful kingdom where you will never be an outsider again.

Gotta go; Blackie needs his supper. Wonder if he likes spaghetti? I know I do.

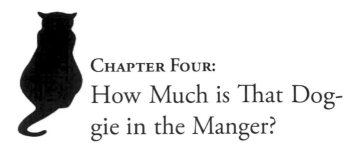

Chapter Four:
How Much is That Doggie in the Manger?

And he said to him, 'Son, you have always been with me,
and all that is mine is yours.'

- Luke 15:31 (NASB)

I do not wish to brag, but it appears I'm going to anyway. It seems that I am a person of some importance. How, you ask with a roll of the eyes, can I make such an outrageously arrogant claim? Simple, I am a confidant of royalty, and they don't consort with everyday commoners such as yourselves. Oil does not mix with water, and Royals do not mix with rabble.

You see, just the other day I received a personal email from a Nigerian prince who was in need of a place to store some of his vast resources. Apparently, there were certain circumstances going on in his country that made it impossible to hold these funds under his own name. I am not sure he ever made it clear what those circumstances were or how he came to contact me personally, but those are matters of little note. He needed help so naturally he would turn to a person he could trust to the uttermost, such as myself, to help him solve his problem. He needed a place to stash some cash, and my bank account was a perfect vehicle to do just that. All I need do is provide him with my bank account numbers, and he will do the rest. What could possibly go wrong? What do you mean "Scam?" Hey, I think I know a scam when I see one.

While we're on the subject of scams, I must admit that when Blackie first arrived outside my door, I thought there was a distinct possibility that he was scamming me and that he probably lived close by and saw me as an easy target for an extra meal or two. I half-way expected that the neighbors would come pounding on my door some morning to demand that I stop feeding their cat, which had now ballooned to forty pounds.

I'll call Blackie a male, but I am really not sure of that gender designation. I can't get close enough to see, and I don't think the image of me chasing a cat down the street trying to get a close up look at its' rear end is one the neighbors would approve of.

Blackie wore no tags or collar. He was well kept, and while thin, he was not scrawny. His fur was orderly and free from burrs and stickers. But as the days and now months have passed, I came to the obvious conclusion that he has no home.

Blackie has no spot on the couch that catches the afternoon sun just right for napping. He has no lap to curl up in. He has no hands to ruffle his fur and none to smooth it carefully afterwards. He has no one to love him. Nothing, absolutely nothing, should go through this life without someone to love them.

Blackie did not keep to any routine that one would expect of a house cat used to roaming at night. He was there before dawn; he was there in the afternoon. He was there rain or shine. He would show up in the middle of a fierce thunderstorm when any cat that had a safe, warm house and three squares a day would be home under the bed. As he got used to my work schedule, he adjusted his time of arrival so he would be there just as I got home.

He would let me get no closer than fifteen feet or so before panic set in, and he took off at the fly. His mistrust of me told me that he trusted no one in his life and that he had no home or family to call his own. Well, I would be his family even if it were a long distance relationship. I would show him that while the world can be a cruel place, he could trust me not to hurt him.

I bought a large bag of cheap cat food. The kind Kolby wouldn't touch if his very life depended on it. I put out a bowl every morning and in the evening when needed.

Kolby could not help but notice what was going on. He saw me put food out, and when I brought in the empty bowls he could smell the scent of another cat. He was not happy. He became suspicious of my movements. He followed me to the kitchen to see if I was going to open the kitchen door. If I put down his food bowl and made any sort of movement toward the outside door, he would leave his dish and run after me, beating me to the door and attempting to block my path. If I put down Blackie's bowl of food long enough to open the door, Kolby would run to it and start eating furiously, thinking if he ate it all first there would be nothing for Blackie. It was almost laughable the lengths to which he went to try and keep me from feeding that "outsider" cat.

One afternoon, Blackie arrived for dinner, and I decided it was time Kolby see his new "brother." Up until this point, Kolby had never caught a glimpse of Blackie. He knew him only through sense of smell. That was about to change.

I opened the door to allow him to see Blackie through the storm window, and he went ballistic. He was hissing and growling. He was all puffed up and had his back arched so high I could have driven a truck under his stomach (technically this is not true. He couldn't arch his back high enough to get his stomach off the ground). He was moaning softly and then suddenly yowling at the top of his lungs.

I was taken completely by surprise. In the three years we had spent together, the only time he had shown anger with another animal was when friends had brought over their little dog, Chico (see my other book for the hilarious details). Even then, he had never acted like this. Now he was out of control.

He stood at the door howling as if his leg was in a trap. It was an eerie mixture of hate and anguish that would raise the hairs on the back of your neck. It went on for long minutes and showed no sign of abating anytime soon.

I came up by his side to try and move him away from the door so I could close it and stem the noise that I'm sure had the neighbors heading to their basements thinking the city had set off the tornado siren. He turned and hissed at me. At me! His Mommy! Oh! The agony caused a mother's heart by an ungrateful child!

I put out my foot to gently nudge him from his position. This was not a good decision on my part. I was wearing my slippers so had very little protection on the upper part of my foot, and when I touched Kolby's side, he turned in an instant and buried his teeth in the top of my foot.

The blood came immediately along with a yelp of pain from me. At once, he seemed to realize what he had done. He disengaged from my foot and did a crab walk into the dining room, hissing and spitting as he went and telling me as plainly as he could that this whole mess was entirely my fault. "Bad Kitty! Bad Kolby!" I yelled limping after him. Bad kitty indeed, more like Jack the Ripper kitty. I count myself fortunate he didn't have a knife.

I hobbled upstairs to wash and dress the bite. I was concerned most about possible infection. With diabetes, I have poor circulation in my feet and am very protective of them. I wish to avoid injury to my feet at all costs as this could set in motion a chain of events that would end up in me losing one foot, or both or in the worst case scenario, all three (Ha, ha, just a funny joke to break the tension).

Upon washing off the blood, I saw three gashes his teeth had left. While they were not as deep as I had originally thought,

a lovely multi-colored bruise was already forming in a three inch radius around the wounds. I hit the cuts with some disinfectant, screamed like a little girl for a few seconds, stuck on some band aids and pulled on a clean sock. Kolby was nowhere to be seen which was just as well for him.

An hour later, I sat at the computer, my injured foot

resting on the desk, absorbed in the game I was playing. From the floor, I heard a soft mew. Kolby had come in silently and was sitting at the foot of the chair.

"Go away! " I said. "You are a bad, bad cat." He lowered his head, meowed and looked up hopefully. "No, you are not getting up here. I'm mad at you." Another soft mew. Turns out I'm not made of stone. "All right," I conceded, "come on up." He jumped in my lap and curled up. "You know," I told him, "if my foot gets infected and I die, you'll end up back at the shelter waiting for some other dumb sap to give you a home. Probably get picked by some guy who expects you to earn your keep by catching mice. We both know how that would turn out, don't we?" He purred contentedly.

Weeks later, at the vet for Kolby's yearly shots, I told the doctor of the incident. He called it "transference." Kolby wasn't mad at me directly. He was mad at Blackie. It was Blackie he wanted to bite, but since he could not get at him, and I was handy, he bit me instead. Well, lucky me. I should just go out now and buy a fistful of lottery tickets.

The story of the Prodigal Son is probably one of the best-known stories in the Bible. It is the compelling story of a rather spoiled young man who is tired of living under his father's tent and has begun to chafe under his father's rules. So he confronts the father and demands his share of whatever money would come his way when the father dies. This is a lovely sentiment in and of itself. "Hey, Dad, how much am I worth once you're dead?"

With this ready cash, he goes off to see the world. He wants everything life can offer. He wants fast friends, fast women and fast camels (no cars back then). He wants parties and sleeping late and no responsibilities. He wants to live, baby! If it feels good, do it!

Well, as one can imagine, the money gave out pretty quickly, and his fast friends left him even faster. The women no longer found him nearly as attractive as when he had a pocket full of jingle. The repo men came and hauled off the flashy two-seater sports camel he had been leasing from "Crazy Akbar's RV and Camel Showroom." From there it just got worse until he found himself fighting the pigs he was tending for the chance to gnaw on a bare old corn cob.

At this point, he wised up and decided to go home and apologize for his treatment of his dad and beg for a second chance. Meanwhile, back at the ranch, the father had been patiently waiting for the return of his son. Every day he went to the gates of his property and spent the time scanning the horizon for the son he had lost. He never gave up hope that this son would someday come home. One day his hopes were realized when he saw his son walking home.

The boy was dirty and smelled like the pigs he had been living with. His clothes were tattered and torn. But to the father, no sight was quite as beautiful as that of his dirty, smelly son.
So they threw a big welcome home party. They feasted they sang, they partied like it was 1999.

Usually this is where we end the story and direct the reader's attention to the obvious analogy that God is the father in the story, and we are the son. But there is another son in this tale. The "other" brother is the good son. He's the older brother who has always done as his father asked. He is the one who never gave his father any cause for concern or embarrassment. He tows the line and honors his father on the surface while deep down he is smoldering with resentment toward his little brother who seems to get all the attention.

Now, after assuming that he had seen the last of this pampered brother of his, here he turns up again like a bad penny and not only does his father forgive the brat; he also throws him the biggest bash the family has seen. This is the last straw.

He refuses to attend the party or even see his brother. His father leaves the tent and goes to him where the older son unloads all the frustrations he had with his brother right onto his father. All the best clichés are there. It's not fair. You never gave me a party. You love him more than me and on and on.

It's called "transference." Although this young man, let's call him Kolby, had everything he could have wanted or desired, he lashes out to hurt the father because of his anger with Blackie, er…I mean his brother.

Rather than rejoice and be glad that his brother had not only returned but also had changed into a better person; he was angry and would have much rather seen his brother dead. In short, he's mad that his father is a loving, forgiving man.

Have you ever been mad at God because of his treatment of you? I have.

In our anger and frustration with life, we lash out at God. We blame Him for all the things that go wrong in our lives. Why did this terrible thing happen to us? Couldn't God have stopped it? He obviously loves others more than us. He doesn't answer when we call. That guy got more blessings than me and I happen to know for sure he's a jerk! And on and on.

Is it OK to be mad at God? Greater minds than mine have pondered this question and cannot come to consensus. Let me toss in my two cents. I say we would not be human if we were not mad at God sometimes. We don't understand His dealings with us and it is frustrating.

Kolby does not understand my dealings with Blackie. He views it as a betrayal on my part. He questions why I would even involve myself with another cat. He cannot see any good that could come of it. He can't reason it through or divine my thoughts on the subject.

"For just as the sky is higher than the earth, so my deeds are superior to your deeds and my plans superior to your plans." Isaiah 55:9 (NET). We often cry out as did the child's father in Mark 9:24 (NLT), "I do believe, but help me overcome my unbelief!" God understands our frail nature and human emotions. He often cuts us some slack when it comes to questioning His decisions. Just don't make it a habit. I know from experience that road has a lot of potholes in it and eventually one will swallow you.

Obviously, the feelings of resentment exhibited by the

older brother in our story had been building for some time until like a volcano they exploded at the father. How much better would it have been for him to visit with the father about his feelings quietly and calmly before he let them destroy the relationship he had with his dad?

"Please come, and let's reason together," implores the Lord." Isaiah 1:18 (ISV). Let's talk about it before it becomes an issue between us, says God.

Kolby cannot reason with me regarding his anger and frustration. He shows it the only way he can. As my friends remind me almost daily, "he's just a cat; he's not people." We, however, can meet with God whenever we are depressed or stressed or frustrated and talk it out. He doesn't mind at all.

Excuse me, there's the phone ringing just now. Sorry, but I have to take the call. It's probably the bank calling to tell me how much money that Nigerian prince just put in my account.

CHAPTER FIVE:
Nobody Nose My Sorrow

*And he said; 'Let me go, for the day breaks.' And he said,
'I will not let you go, except you bless me.'*
- Genesis 32:26 (AKJV)

When I was little, I had a stuffed bear as my bed buddy. Whether it was nap-time or night-time, I never went to sleep without him. He was a dear friend until the day I got sick suddenly and threw up all over him. No matter how many times my mother scrubbed poor Bear, she could not wash away his shame. As a result, our bear/child relationship was never quite the same. I lost a little of my innocence, and Bear went to live in the attic. It was all very sad.

Now, I have an eighteen pound cat as a bed buddy. It must have something to do with the laws of physics because I sure cannot explain how something roughly the size of a shoe box can manage to take up an entire queen-sized bed. It's like sharing a bed with the Jolly Green Giant. That reminds me, how come you never see the Jolly Green Giant anymore? He used to be on TV all the time. I'm guessing he must be pretty old by now and is in some Hollywood rest home for aging advertising mascots. I can see him now as he rocks on the porch and reminisces with Speedy Alka Seltzer.

Speedy: "I tell ya, Jolly Green, there was a time when 'plop-plop, fizz-fizz' meant something in this town."
Jolly Green Giant: "Ho, ho, zzzzzzz."

Where was I? Oh yes, sleeping with a bed-hogging cat. Kolby has this night-time routine he follows most every evening. It will begin just about the time I am ready to close my book and turn off the light.

I am what is known in the professional world of Polysomnography (spell-check about blew a gasket with that one) as a "side-sleeper." I do not sleep on my back. I can't even begin to relate to tummy-sleepers. To me you might as well be buried alive as sleep on your stomach with your face mashed into the pillow. But to each his own I say, no matter how depraved. I normally start out on my left side with my back to the doorway. As I said, about the time I'm ready to douse the light, Kolby comes in the door. He jumps on the bed and sits there looking over my shoulder to be sure I have spread out the blankets in front of me and left room for him to make a nice cozy nest to curl up in. If I have done a sufficiently competent job of blanket smoothing, he then proceeds to walk over me one paw at a time and settle in about level with my chest. I don't know why he doesn't just walk around the bed and jump directly into his spot. I suppose that by walking over me, he is probably sending some type of subliminal message about who is actually in charge of the relationship.

Once he has reached the Promised Land, he sits down and starts to knead the blankets. My mother always said that when a cat did this he was "making bread." For you young Gen Xers (I don't think that's right. What letter of the alphabet are we on now to describe the current generation?), there was a time when people made their own bread. It was very hard work and the dough had to be poked and prodded and punched and patted just right, or the bread came out tough. In retrospect, this overt, housewifely-aggression against flour and yeast probably saved many a marriage in the 1950s.

As he is kneading the blankets, he starts to purr. Kolby has a very unusual purr. It's rather wheezy, and I imagine it sounds a lot like how a long-time smoker would sound if they could purr. He takes in big gulps of air when he is purring, and sooner or later this air has to find a way back out of his stomach. So he burps. If you have never heard a cat burp before, you would enjoy hearing Kolby. He burps loud and often. It's very impressive. I've got a video on my computer of him burping and if I could figure out how to do it, I would post it to the internet (where's a Gen Xer when you need one?).

Anyhoo, the other night he was kneading and wheezing and purring and burping and having a grand old time when his nose started to run. Soon, he had a big glistening droplet hanging precariously off the end. And it wouldn't let go! It just hung there wobbling with his every movement. Like a rubber-necker at a train wreck, I could not look away. I am only a foot or so away from the action, and I just lay there mesmerized waiting for it to drop. But it won't let go.

Any other time, Kolby is as fastidious as a Victorian-era Fop, but this time he seemed completely oblivious to what's going on, in the most literal sense, right under his nose. So I figure maybe I'll help it along a little. I reach out cautiously from under the blankets and give him a little shove hoping that will dislodge it. Nope, it's still there. I shove him again. No dice. It won't let go. Meanwhile, he keeps on purring and kneading. Then I think maybe if I tap the back of his head that may do the trick. So I reach out and gently pat him on the top of the head. *Pat, pat, pat, PAT!* The only thing that happens is he shoots me a dirty look all the while the drop swings to and fro on the end of his nose like Jell-O in a hurricane. It simply won't let go.

Well, there's only one thing left to do. Get up, go in the bathroom and get a piece of tissue, come back to bed and wipe his nose. But as is too often the case, doing the right thing takes way too much effort. Why go to all that bother? I'm comfy and warm right now. Does that need to change? Instead, I reach out to gather in the very farthest corner of the blanket. The part that doesn't matter what gets on it because I never touch it anyway (Oh, now, don't gasp in disgust. You know what YOU do when you're home all alone). Besides, I promise myself, I'll wash it soon.

My plan is to take this distant corner of the blanket and dab his nose dry. That's the plan anyway. As he sees the blanket coming toward him, he jerks his head out of the way. Does this sudden movement cause the drop to fall? No, it won't let go! Now I realize this is going to be a two-hand task. I reach out with one hand and grab his head to hold it still. With the other, I cram the blanket in his face and rub. Gottcha! Finally! We can rest. *BURRRP!*

Abraham's two grandsons were born just seconds apart but, you would never know they were twins by looking at them. Jacob was fair and an introvert who preferred to stay at home. Esau was hairy and an outdoorsman more at home hunting in the wilds than staying in the tent. Jacob was spiritual; Esau was not. Jacob was thoughtful and introspective. Esau was feckless and impulsive. Whenever I think of Jacob and Esau, I think of Michael and Sonny Corleone from *The Godfather* (minus the Tommy guns of course).

As the second born, Jacob strongly coveted the blessing that the firstborn would receive. This blessing was not only an earthly inheritance of money and possessions, but also represented the continuation of the covenant God had established with Abraham, whose descendants were to hold a special place in the redemptive plan of the Lord. This was the part of the blessing that Jacob coveted. He knew that Esau couldn't care less about this blessing, and it galled Jacob to see it go to someone so undeserving. Still, he knew that his father, Isaac, was bound by tradition and law to bestow his blessing upon Esau whether he wanted to or not.

Here, Jacob made a great mistake. Rather than wait and let God work things out, he and his mother, Rebekah, conspired to obtain the blessing by fraud and deception. Together they made Isaac an offer he couldn't refuse (venison...Isaac loved him some venison). The plan was successful but at the same time backfired terribly and Jacob ended up fleeing his home before Esau could hunt him down and extract his pound of flesh.

Jacob spent many years running from his brother and his own guilty conscience. Nevertheless, he fared well in his exile and became a wealthy family man. After a while, Jacob came to feel true repentance for what he had done and, with a nudge from the Lord, decided it was time to go home and take his medicine, whatever medicine he had waiting. On his way home, he sent peace emissaries to plead with his brother. Then, he heard that Esau and a host of his fiercest fighters were coming out to meet him. This was terrible news that most likely meant his peace offerings had been rejected. Esau was a warrior; Jacob was a homebody. It would be a slaughter.

That night, Jacob sent his family across the river to safety. He remained alone and in great mental anguish. Was Esau on his way to kill him? Had God truly forgiven him? Would his own sin now result in the deaths of his innocent family? He needed answers, but they weren't coming.

As he knelt, seeking God's guidance, he felt a hand grip his shoulder. Fearing it might be an assassin sent by Esau, he jumped at the man, and they began to struggle with each other. Seemingly all night they grappled together with neither one able to get the upper hand. As morning broke, the man reached down and touched Jacob's hip. It immediately became dislocated. Wowchie! I dislocated one of my little piggies once (if I remember right it was the one who had roast beef) and boy howdy, did that hurt. I can't imagine the pain of a dislocated hip.

At that point, Jacob realized that he was not wrestling against flesh and blood, but he was wrestling with God, both physically and metaphorically. At once, he stopped trying to overcome the Man and instead just wrapped his arms around Him and held on for dear life. "Let me go," the Man said. "I will not let go," Jacob sobbed. "Not until you bless me."

Poor Jacob. He's riddled with guilt, broken emotionally, spiritually spent, physically exhausted and in unbearable pain, yet he hangs on to the Lord with all that he has left and begs for a blessing. "I won't let you go," he declares. He has nobody else to cling to.

At some time in our lives, events will conspire to try and force us to let loose our hold on God. We have an Adversary who, as a "roaring lion" is looking for ways to cut us off from our only source of power. And he is good at it. He will find our weakness and burrow deep into our souls like a hungry termite eating into the support beams of a house, hoping if he burrows deep enough, the house will collapse.

I was born a musician. Both my parents had musical talent, and I guess they passed it on to me. My interest lay dormant until I was in Jr. High (I refuse to refer to it as middle school. What am I, a hobbit?). I went over to a friend's house and heard him play a wobbly version of the Ventures' hit, "Pipeline" on his brand new Fender Mustang guitar, and that was all it took. I started playing guitar and by the time I was in my mid-twenties, I played ten fretted/string instruments at a professional level. It just came natural to me. I had plans and dreams about my future and what role music would play in it. This was going to be my life.

Then one morning when I woke up, my right hand no longer did what I was asking it to do. My fingers curled into a ball all of their own accord. I had sustained no injury. The hand looked perfectly normal, but it had a mind of its' own now. The simplest of tasks were very difficult. I was clumsy and had no dexterity. When it came to playing an instrument, I couldn't.

I went to a doctor. He had no answers. I'm a pretty high-strung guy and demand perfection from myself at all times so I tried relaxation techniques thinking it may be a psychological issue. Nope. I did strength and conditioning exercises. Nothing worked. Eventually, I had to learn to play all over again using different fingers and different techniques. It took years before I became proficient again, but I was never as good as I had been and had no real hope of progressing any further than the level I had been able to return to. Some instruments, such as the banjo, were lost to me for good, and I never could recover. This was a terrible pill to swallow as I loved playing bluegrass banjo best of all.

Many years later, a friend gave me an article about something called Focal Dystonia that sounded an awful lot like what I was dealing with. Focal Dystonia is a distant cousin to Parkinson's disease. Its deepest impact is on muscle memory movements. These are the reflexive movements we make without really thinking. Unlike mine, the normal brain is a marvel of efficient multi-tasking. While consciously your brain is making important life-decisions such as whether to leave the onions off your burger or if that new pair of shoes is necessary (according to my wife, they are), subliminally it is running the machine that is your body. Like breathing and blinking, the brain guides your movements and actions without the distraction of conscious thought. Picking up a pen, typing on a keyboard, drumming your fingers on the table, these are all performed by muscle memory and take no thought on our part.

With Focal Dystonia, the brain short-circuits and begins to send out the wrong message to certain muscles. These muscles become confused and cannot perform the tasks they once did with ease. The hand cannot pick up a pen anymore as it has forgotten how to do so (as an interesting side note, in the days before medicine had a name for this condition, it was known as "writer's cramp" as it most often affected the hands of writers). These disruptions can impact many specific areas of the body. In my case, it was my right hand only.

My brain, instead of telling my hand to open, now tells it to close. If you wish to shake my hand, I have to make a conscious decision to extend my hand in the open position. If I just stick out my hand to you without thinking about that action, I will give you a fist. It's crazy all right. Up is down, black is white, in is out. Forget it, Jake; it's Chinatown!

I went to the Mayo Clinic in Rochester, Minnesota for diagnosis and confirmation. Gradually the ailment spread to my left hand and progressed to the point that, once again, I could no longer perform. The last time I ever played in public was at the funeral of my wife's grandfather in 1999. After bumbling through such an important moment, I knew then, that was it.

Perhaps the worst part of it all was the loss of identity I suffered. I was a musician. This defined me and everything I undertook. It bound me to other musicians. While I never sought it out, it brought me adulation and admiration. I knew that in this life, there was something I could excel at, and that gave me confidence. When that ability was gone, I no longer knew who I was.

I will be honest here and tell you I spent many years blaming God for taking away the thing I loved most. I lost one of the few things that brought me joy in this bleak old world. Outwardly, I seemed unchanged. I still went to church faithfully. I supported His work with my tithe and offerings. I taught the classes and preached the sermons and visited the sick and encouraged the discouraged, but it never went to my heart. Just as the crew of the Titanic, I was busy helping people into the lifeboat knowing all the while that there was no seat for me.

I guess I was that drop on Kolby's nose, just hanging there serving no real purpose and only waiting for the inevitable fall into oblivion. What God had put upon me was too hard. I wanted to say goodbye to Him and just not worry about it anymore. But I, like Jacob, had nowhere else to go. Once you've known God, there is nothing in this life to fall back on that will bring you any peace or comfort. For a little while, perhaps you can find satisfaction. As the Bible says, there is pleasure in this world for a season. But it won't last.

For His part, God refused to wipe me away. He could just

as easily have taken a corner of the blanket to blot me out of His master plan, but He didn't. He waited patiently, never left me, and eventually brought me back to Him through the sage counsel of a minister many years my junior who was able to give me a perspective I had been unable to see before.

There's a popular saying that opines: "If you love something, let it go." This is a wonderful sentiment for schmaltzy love songs and chick flicks, but it has no place in our relationship with the Lord. In fact, His advice is just the opposite. When you find the Kingdom, never let it go. No matter what it takes, do not let go! Here's what Jesus had to say about it: "Again, the Kingdom of Heaven is like a merchant on the lookout for choice pearls. When he discovered a pearl of great value, he sold everything he owned and bought it!" Matthew 13:45,46 (NLT). If you've found that pearl, hug it tight.

I'll miss music every single day of my life from here till the end. I don't listen to it much on the radio. I don't buy CDs or listen to my old recordings very often. It's too painful. However, I now realize the Kingdom is worth every physical pain, every heartache, every relationship dissolved, every dream shattered. God is not oblivious to our hurt. Our lives of trouble and sorrow do not give Him pleasure. He hurts along with us, but he is working out our salvation, and whatever is needed to accomplish that, He will do. In a verse that I now find particularly applicable to me, Jesus says, "So if your hand causes you to lose your faith, cut it off!" Mark 9:43 (GWT). Jesus is certainly not advocating self-mutilation here, but He is saying that nothing should come between us in our quest for the Kingdom. Perhaps music would have led me on a path far away from God. The world of music has seduced many others who had greater talent and more intelligence than me and, as a result, they have lost their lives.

If my salvation came through the loss of the use of my hands, then so be it. Who am I to complain about that? Should I stand at the foot of the cross, look up at Jesus nailed there and say, "BTW, my hands don't work anymore, and I am very angry with you right now. Are you listening to me? Stop dying for a minute and answer me!"

Here's some simple, straightforward advice from Christ: "Just hold on to what you have until I come." Revelation 2:25 (ISV).

Though the earth around you quakes, don't let go. Though the heart inside you breaks, don't let go. Though it's so dark you have no idea which way is up or which way is out, don't let go. Like Kolby's dew drop, we've got to hold on and not let go. You see, we've got nowhere safe to fall.

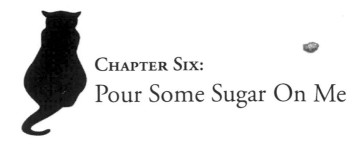

Chapter Six:
Pour Some Sugar On Me

Every good and perfect gift is from above, coming down from the Father.

       - James 1:17 (NIV)

S everal years ago, I was diagnosed with Type II diabetes. This news came out of the blue. I didn't exhibit the classic symptoms, and it was simply by accident that the doctor made the diagnosis.

  I had a bad cold that wouldn't go away, so I did something I rarely do which is seek medical attention. While there, I mentioned that my feet had been burning lately, and it was starting to travel up my legs. The doctor seemed to think this was significant and immediately drew blood for analysis. She came back within a few hours with the news that my A1C (what in the world is that?) was at 11.2. I asked if that was a bad thing. They put me on a high dosage of medication and sent me off to diabetes boot camp where I learned all about what I now had.

Of course, I already knew everything there was to know about diabetes. It was a disease that fat people got because they ate mounds of chocolate and never exercised. I was not overweight (all right, I'll cop to a few extra pounds around the equator but that was just happy fat). My job is not sedentary. I eat very little in the way of sweets. I don't care for ice cream. If Ben and Jerry had to exist on the income generated from my ice cream purchases, they would be living under a bridge in Peoria. I can't stand cake. I'll eat cake at a wedding to be polite or if someone puts a gun to my head, but those are the only two instances. I don't eat much chocolate either. I do like a doughnut every once in a while, but it must be plain no sprinkles and accompanied by a large glass of milk to cut the sweetness.

What I do like to eat in mass quantities are milk, potatoes and bread. I could live on these three comestibles by simply varying their order. Day one: potatoes, milk, bread. Day two: bread, potatoes, milk. Day three: pizza with fries and milk.
At diabetes training, I learned that these three items are loaded with carbs and that carbs…wait for it… are nothing more than sugar looking for a place to happen. So here I was, blissful in my ignorance thinking I was immune to any disease caused by too much sugar because I was a good boy who didn't eat sugar. Poets have a word to describe such a person as myself: putz.

Here's the deal as I see it. Sugar is the fuel that runs your body. It is the oil that lubes the machine. The match that provides the spark to the TNT. The…well I can't think of any other clever metaphors.

You body is a sugar making fool. Basically everything you eat is turned into sugar. Inside you, there is a little work crew. The foreman of this crew determines what to do with the food as it comes in. It works like this:

Crew member number one: "We're getting in a load of pancakes and hash browns."

Foreman: "Make it into sugar and send it to the thighs."

Crew member number two: "Boss we've got an apple on

the way down."

Foreman: "Sugar."

Crew member number three: "Hey, what are we going to do with this lettuce?"

Foreman (checking his manifest): "We didn't order this! Run it on through ASAP." (This is much better than the alternative action your body sometimes takes, which is to send it back the way it came.)

Since I've learned how to deal with diabetes, I am keeping my blood sugar levels low and getting along fine with the exception that I have developed a case of diabetic neuropathy in my feet that leaves me walking on two swollen painful cabbages at times. But it is what it is, and I am learning, just like Paul, in all things to be content (or at the very least, to keep my trap shut).

One very interesting side effect though is that I now eat much more in the way of sweets than I ever ate before. I find that, with me, my blood sugars in the morning can run very high even though I haven't eaten since the night before. That's because my liver likes to stay up at night and make extra sugar just in case I might find myself stranded on a remote desert island. My liver must be a Boy Scout as it likes to be prepared. The only way I can counteract this is to eat a piece of candy or something sugary right before bed. This shuts down the sugar making process for the night and leaves my levels nearer normal come morning. This also means I am eating candy every day like it or not.

To vary this routine, I sometimes buy a small bottle of pure maple syrup and pour myself a spoonful at bedtime. I do like pure maple syrup (strangely enough though, not on pancakes), and while it is expensive, I can buy a 3oz. bottle at the grocery store for a couple of bucks and it's enough for quite a few spoonfuls. And thus we get to Kolby (Reader: *it's about time. I thought this book was about a cat, not about you complaining about your feet*).

One night as I poured myself a treat, Kolby decided that this looked like something he could find very interesting. I don't know if it was the look, the smell or my boisterous lip smacking that first drew his attention but once he had determined this looked like a good thing he was not going to be deterred. He had convinced himself he needed this. This was going to be the best thing that had happened to him since he found that cheese curl under the couch. He had to have this. He could not live without it. So he parked his bulk at my feet and started his supplications, and there was nothing I could do to dissuade him.

"Kitty, you won't like this."
Meow.
"This is sticky sweet, you don't like sticky sweet."
Meow, meow.
"You have all kinds of good food in your bowl."
Meow, meow, meow!
"LEAVE ME ALONE!
MEOW, MEOW, MEOW!!!

Finally, I had had enough. I put a finger over the bottle top and wet it with syrup. Then I bent down for him to sniff. Two things happened simultaneously. One, he decided right away it was nothing he wanted. Two, in bending down, I tipped the bottle sideways and spilled the syrup all over him. It was all over his back. Running down his fur. Dripping on the kitchen floor.

For an instant, he froze. What was this terrible sensation? It was wet and not wet all at the same time. Then he decided the best way to deal with the issue was to run like the wind. Away he went. Into the living room, he ran at top speed, through the sun room, back into the dining room, and under the table. I found him there licking the syrup off his fur. From the face he made after every pass of his tongue I knew he was not enjoying this one bit. It was not the treat he thought it would be. He was sorry he had ever asked for a taste because now he was getting all he could handle, and it was just awful.

Days later, I could still feel the residue clinging to his fur. It was kind of like petting fly paper. Never again did he beg me

for a taste of maple syrup. In fact, several days after the incident, I was pouring a spoonful when he came in the kitchen. The minute he saw the bottle; he ran into the living room (here I must admit I chased after him, bottle in hand.) The last I saw of him he was squeezing his big bottom under the couch (as a follow up to the above, over a year after the incident, he has forgotten the bottle but not the smell. If he gets a whiff of maple syrup he's out of the kitchen in a flash). Kolby had been on the wrong end of a classic "be careful what you wish for" moment.

In the Bible, we can find another good example of this old maxim. The Israelites lived under a theocracy. This means that God, not a human, was their leader. But as they looked at the nations around them they decided it would be a much better form of government to have an actual king. They were determined to blend in with their surroundings no matter the cost. So they petitioned the Lord to find them a king. God told them this was not a good idea. But they insisted. God told them a king would take their young men to war just so he could expand his territory.

But they insisted. God said a king will cost you money, and he will tax you to pay for his lavish lifestyle. But they insisted. Finally, God found them just the kind of king they had been asking for, and you know what? It didn't work out too well. Everything God said would happen did happen. By the time of Solomon's reign, it was costing the nation a small fortune just to feed his household. For fun, look up First Kings 4:20-28 and see what supplies were needed to feed Solomon's household every day. It is much more than even Kolby can eat.

God is very good at answering our prayers. The problem is we are not very good at knowing what to ask for. I remember when I was 15 and on the verge of getting my driver's license, a local supermarket was giving away a motorcycle. It was a 50cc Honda Dream. A small putt-putt bike but to me at the time it was like a Harley chopper. I wanted to win that bike bad. So I prayed about it.

Not only did I make it a permanent part of my nightly petitions, I went to every adult I knew and had them fill out an entry slip (I was too young to enter). I had more than 50 entries in that cardboard box. All those entries, along with biblical assurances that what I asked for in faith I would receive, led me to believe that the motorcycle was as good as mine. Then came the day of the drawing. I did not win.

James gave us a reason why our prayers go unanswered. "You ask and do not receive, because you ask wrongly, to spend it on your passions." James 4:3 (ESV). Our prayers are mostly selfish. Even the good ones. Our needs, our wants, are sometimes all we think about when Jesus told us to seek the Kingdom first, and then these other things would come.

The obvious conclusion is that we need to learn to pray in such a way that God's desires become our desires. It seems logical to me, if we can bring our will in line with God's, our prayers should have a much better chance of success. But what about those times we have done just that and our prayers are still seemingly ignored?

In the late 1980s, after the fall of communism, the floodgates opened in Russia for the gospel to be preached. I had friends, a husband and wife, who moved to Moscow to help work in the newly opened mission field. They shared with me the following story:

A young minister they knew had two churches to shepherd in two small rural towns about eight miles apart. He did not have a car so he would often just walk the distance. Usually, he could catch a ride with someone who had a car. It was pretty common for folks who had vehicles to pick up a hitch hiker and take them along. The hitcher would give the driver a few rubles for the ride, and it worked out good for everyone.

One winter day, the pastor had a church meeting to attend in the next town. He started walking down the road figuring he would catch a ride quickly. Soon a car came along but when he signaled the driver to stop, the car just sped on past. OK, well, someone else would get him then. It started to snow, and the temperatures started to drop. Another car came down the road at a brisk pace. Again it paid no attention to him as he tried to wave it down.

Now he was becoming concerned. He was too far out to turn around and too far from the next town to get there safely on foot. If someone did not stop for him, he was in trouble. The snow fell faster and heavier. The air got colder. So he offered up a prayer. He had prayed, as he always did, when starting his journey, but now his prayer had a greater sense of urgency.

After a few minutes, a third car came speeding along. He waved and shouted and watched as the car drove by. He was now numb with cold. He could no longer feel his feet, and he was getting sleepy. And his prayers were going unanswered. Here he was out in the dangerous elements going about the Lord's business and for his trouble he might end up stiff as a board in a frozen Russian field.

Just then a fourth car came slowly down the road. This was an old beat up rattley-trap car driven by an old beat up rattley-trap man. The pastor waved. The car stopped.

Jumping inside the car, the heat was wonderful. The old man drove off. As he began to warm back to normal, the pastor started thinking less about survival and more about his meeting. He was going to be very late, and this old guy was driving slower than a turtle on valium. Rather than be thankful he was safe and warm, he now began to question why the old guy couldn't drive a little faster. Couldn't God have sent him someone who could exert a tad more pressure on the gas pedal?

Soon they arrived at the bottom of a small hill. Sputtering to the top, the old man pulled to the side of the road and got out to assess the situation. The minister got out as well. As they looked down the road, there, at the bottom of the hill, were the three cars that had passed him by earlier. Each of them was upside down in the ditch.

When God answers our prayers, He sees so much farther down the road than we do. We pray in the here and now and God answers with an eye in the future. God has one overriding purpose in His dealings with us, and that is to get us to heaven. He will do whatever it takes to accomplish this task. Sometimes that involves a painful experience.

I have always hated having to get a shot at the doctor's. I am not afraid of needles, but I don't like the idea of that thing going in my arm or the resultant pain. When I was little, my mom would bribe me with popcorn from the candy store just down the block from the doctor's office. If I was a brave little trooper and did not kick the Doctor's shins, I got freshly popped and heavily buttered popcorn. So I would man up and tough it out.

Now that I have to have my blood drawn what seems like every other day, I try to sit still and not fidget or squirm because usually there is a pretty girl drawing the blood, and I don't want her to see me as anything less than brave and stalwart. Sometimes, in a show of bravado, I ask her to use an even bigger needle because I can take it (this is a complete untruth, and I can't believe I would tell such a whopper).

My point is the pain is for my own good. I would rather not have to give my blood for testing or stick my finger every day to check my sugars but for my own safety and long term health I have to.

There are many things in this life we would rather not go through if given the option, but they are good for us. They build character and faith. Both of which will serve us in good stead in the future.

Jesus said ask, seek and knock. Ask for an understanding of God's will for your life. Seek to be like Him. Knock on heaven's door, and it will be opened that we may see God more clearly. Rather than be frustrated, angry, discouraged or lose heart when our prayers go unanswered, maybe we need to reassess exactly what we are asking for.

There is one prayer that you can offer up at any time, and it will always receive an immediate and affirmative answer. That prayer is simply, "Lord, teach me more about you. Let me learn at your feet and become more like you every day." This prayer makes God smile. This is the prayer He has been waiting for.

So take this advice from your old fuzzy-faced pal Kolby, who can tell you from experience that the spoonful of syrup you've been begging for may not be the cat's meow after all.

Chapter Seven:
Oops! I Did It Again!

*The Lord will rescue me from every evil deed and bring
me safely into His heavenly kingdom.*
                    - Second Timothy 4:18 (NLT)

At the very least, having Blackie come into his life has given
Kolby a purpose. It has brought his rather meandering
lifestyle into sharply defined focus. He has a *raison d'être*
if you will.

In short it has given him the one thing he seemed to be
lacking: an enemy. And not just any enemy, a "mortal" enemy.

I doubt that Blackie would describe their relationship in
this fashion but as nobody is asking his opinion that hardly has
any bearing on the matter. The fact is Kolby now has an enemy,
and one which must be guarded against with all-encompassing
vigil.

I am a child of the "Duck & Cover" days of the 1960s
when we all thought that a school desk covered on the underside

{ Kolby has applied to work for the TSA to check for smuggled }
{ cats, but their benefits (read: treats) program is deplorable. }

with used chewing gum could protect us against all out nuclear assault. I remember the tense days of the Cuban missile crisis. Just as the United States kept a close watch on Cuba for any sign of imminent threat to its national security, so Kolby keeps an eye out for Blackie.

The kitchen door is the nexus between the two cats. More specifically, it is on the slight gap where door meets jamb that Kolby focuses. This gap provides him an opportunity to put his nose as close to the crack as he can get and then draw in deep breaths to see if he can get an idea if Blackie is in close proximity and what threat level alert he needs to issue. For the most part, Kolby has adopted and adapted the threat assessment chart developed by US Homeland Security. Green for low (unruffled fur), Yellow for elevated (puffy tail only), Orange for high alert (full body puff) and Red for "my head's about to bus' open!"

I believe that Kolby honestly thinks he is protecting not

only his own home and hearth, but he is watching out for me too. He thinks I am not seeing the big picture here. He does not understand how I can have such a blasé attitude when danger lurks just outside the door. Though I have explained to him countless times that Blackie presents no threat to him, his lifestyle or his master and that the poor thing is just trying to survive in a tough old world, the words only whistle in one pointy ear and out the other.

The kitchen door has become a point of no retreat. Kolby stands, as did the brave 300 Spartans at the pass of Thermopylae, against the overwhelming odds of the mightiest army then known to man. His message to Blackie is loud and clear, "You shall not pass!"

So with nose to the door, Kolby waits...and waits...and waits. Anyone entering the kitchen would think that he had been a bad kitty and, as a result, received a lengthy timeout. Not so, he willingly serves his country on the first line of defense. Often in the middle of the night he will awaken and head downstairs. I know what his itinerary will be. A quick stop at the food bowl, perhaps a jog downstairs for a visit to the litter box; an hour or two of sentry duty, and finally return to bed to rest up for another day of keeping evil at bay.

The other night I was reading in bed when I heard mewing from downstairs. I didn't think much of it as Kolby talks all the time whether or not I am in the room. He has the gift of gab and talks to himself as much as he does to me. A few minutes passed and the tone of the mewing changed ever so slightly. It now held a note of fear. When five minutes had gone by, and he was still meowing, I decided I'd better go see if there was any real cause for concern.

Entering the kitchen, I flipped the light switch on to find Kolby standing on top of the refrigerator. What! How on earth he got up there is still a mystery to me (I haven't ruled out some sort of teleportation at this point). The only thing I can figure is he jumped from floor to stove and then from stove to refrigerator.

Still, that's some pretty impressive jumping for an 18 lb. tub of flubby. To top it off, I usually put any recyclables on top of the fridge until I get enough to take outside to the container and at this time there was a plastic milk jug along with 5-6 empty tin cans stacked up on top, and not one of them had been disturbed! Though I can't tell you how he got up there, I can sure tell you why he got up there. The refrigerator stands adjacent to the outside door and from the top he could see down through the windows in the door to the landing where Blackie's food bowl sits. Visual confirmation is a much better way of tracking Blackie than sense of smell. But now he could not get down. He had gotten himself into a terrible fix, and he knew it. He meowed at me and put out a paw asking for my help.

I would like to be able to say that I responded with love and compassion and tenderly rescued him from his situation. That would not be the entire truth. First, I laughed at him (which he did not like). Then I lectured him and told him I was going to leave him up there and he could find his own way down (this was a hollow threat, and he knew it). Then I held out my hands; he leaned into them, and I put him gently on the floor. He has not been on top of the fridge since.

Blackie, for his part, has taken to stopping by the house at all hours looking for food. He will arrive in the early morning before sunup, late at night, or even afternoons. One day I came home from work to find Blackie sitting on the landing next to his empty bowl patiently waiting for supper. I had forgotten to put out any food that morning so I suppose he was very hungry. I put the car away and hurried to the kitchen telling Blackie as I walked past that I would get his supper immediately and not to run away.

In the kitchen, I filled two bowls; one with food and one with water. Seeing that Kolby was not yet downstairs, I opened the kitchen door and hip-bumped the storm door open to put the food on the landing. At once all hallelujah broke loose. A large grey ball of fur that was named Kolby tore through my legs, nearly tripping me and causing the bowl of water to spill down my front.

Blackie, seeing a massive angry hippo closing on him fast turned tail and ran down the sidewalk. Kolby was after him at a rate of speed I did not think he could ever achieve.

They were both past me before I could react, and I stood there knowing I could do nothing about the situation. Terrible scenarios flashed through my head. Kolby does not go outside. Until this very moment, he had never gone outside voluntarily. Here he was speeding down the block after Blackie.

Blackie has street smarts. He knows how to cross the road and how to avoid cars. I've watched him come up to the house. He sits on the curb until all traffic is past before he walks across the street. Kolby has no experience with moving vehicles. If Blackie leads him into the street, he will follow blindly and in all likelihood get hit by a car, leaving me with the lasting memory of my best friend being squashed like a bug on a windshield.

Blackie knows how to navigate outside. A friend of mine told me he once saw him as far as three blocks away apparently on his way toward my house. Kolby would be hopelessly lost if he got as far as a block from home. He would never find his way back. The situation looked bleak.

Suddenly, Kolby realized an important fact that his anger had caused him to overlook. He was outside. And not only was he outside, he was also far from home. You could see the exact moment these thoughts hit him. He stopped dead in his tracks and stood there quivering. It was just like those cartoons where the guy is running at full speed and hits a puddle of glue and comes to a screeching halt. All we were missing was the loud sound effect, *boiiinng!*

Kolby put his head down and began to meow loudly. Blackie kept on going until he was out of sight. I walked over slowly and picked up Kolby. There were no lectures this time. I did not tease him or scold him. I was just thankful he was all right. I carried him home quietly and shut the door.

Much like Kolby, we seem to be very adept at getting ourselves into tricky situations. At least I know I am. Often we make important decisions based upon emotions rather than rational thought. That's the approach to life I call the "Think it-Do it" plan. Often it has disastrous consequences.

My great aunt, late in her life, married a man 25 years her junior who she had known for just over a week. She did this despite the strenuous objections of family and friends. I suppose loneliness played a large part in her motivation, but less than a year later he was gone along with most of her remaining wealth, and she was not only lonely once more but broke, as well. She lost her house and what modest cash reserves she in had place to live on.

In my opinion, she could count herself lucky (or more accurately, blessed) to lose only her possessions for this man took the term "crazy" to dizzying new heights. One day she came home from visiting friends to find the crystal chandelier that hung in her foyer had been painted bright orange. Every tiny crystal fob had been removed, dipped in orange paint and hung back up to dry. Why? Your guess would be as good as ours for we never did know the thought process behind this bizarre gesture other than he said he did it for her.

There are those times too when we do think things through to a certain point, but we get tunnel vision on specific details and fail to see the pitfalls. Then we make another lousy call. Kolby thought he had everything planned out very well to get to the top of the fridge and at least the first part of his plan worked. He just had no exit strategy.

In retrospect, we can see why some of our life decisions are bound to fail. We race ahead of God and pay the price. We have plenty of life advice to be found in the scriptures, but we either fail to read it or fail to heed it. We fail to make God an active partner in our life and the results are not as we hoped.

But what about the times we have carefully considered our life? We have done our best to be sure we are making a quality decision in accordance with God's will. We have prayed over the issue and placed it in God's hands. Then it all goes sour faster than a mayonnaise sandwich on the dashboard in July. These times try our faith like no other. I've been there as I'm sure you have too. The great men and women of the Bible have all had this experience. Jeremiah, Isaiah, Elijah have all felt forsaken and betrayed by God. Even Jesus on the cross had one of these human moments when he cried out, "My God, My God, why have you forsaken me?"

The fact is, in this life, we have no assurance that every event will be a happy or successful one. Somewhere I have a birth certificate that proves I was born and not hatched from an egg or discovered under a mattress in the dump like my sister always postulated. Unfortunately, it does not carry any warranty as to what my life will be like. There is no place I can go to get back the years that have not been particularly good ones. "Hello, I'd like to return 1974, please. It just did not work out."

Not every plan will succeed. Not every dream will be realized. This could be due to poor decision making, faulty planning, unforeseen circumstances or the fact it is simply not God's will for us.

The only ironclad guarantee we have is the one given by God: "For the Lord your God goes with you. He will never leave you or forsake you." Deut. 31:6 (NIV). This is a promise that makes the rest of our existence worthwhile. No matter how far we stray, no matter how low we sink. No matter how many times we fail. Whether our situation is of our own making or beyond our control, the Lord remains faithful.

"And we know that God causes everything to work together for the good of those who love God and are called according to his purpose." Romans 8:28 (NLT). Now there's a promise that I've always struggled with. I've walked through the valley of the shadow so many times that I have a commemorative bench along the path with my name on it. But as many times as I've thought this would be the time I didn't come out the other side, the Lord has always seen me safely through.

When you find yourself in times of trouble, take a tip from Kolby, stop, lower your head and ask God to come to your rescue. He will do it gladly because he loves you. He will lift you up and carry you home.

You may suffer the consequences of your actions, and these may not be pleasant but seeing the Lord work on your behalf will serve to strengthen your faith and teach you to lean more fully on the everlasting arms. And for crying out loud, stay off the refrigerator!

Chapter Eight:
A Little White Lie

There is a path before each person that seems right, but it ends in death.
- Proverbs 16:25 (NLT)

Whoever thought up this whole "re-gifting" thing is a genius and I'd like to shake their hand and follow that up with a good swift kick in the pants. The genius of the idea is what better way to get the junk out of your house and into the house of a friend or neighbor than to "re-gift" it in some manner that makes you seem magnanimous rather than just too plain lazy to load up and go to the dump.

The kick in the pants is deserved because you are often blindsided in return with a "re-gift" of something you didn't want and never asked for. So while you are smiling happily at the clever way you got rid of that awful rainbow colored toaster cozy hand-knit for you by Great Aunt Flora, your neighbor is silently plotting to give you an equally horrid puce colored toilet paper cozy hand-

{ Hardly the stuff of legends. }

knit for them by their Great Aunt Fauna. There are no winners in the re-gifting game, only losers.

Why this rant? Well, once again I have been the recipient of someone else's cast offs. Since I have a cat I talk about a lot, people assume that anything to do with a cat will tickle my fancy. So I get all kinds of cat stuff. Some old and some new. My wife, Kim, bought me a set of cat-butt refrigerator magnets. These magnets are exactly as you visualize; small 3-D plastic backsides of cats that you use to stick notes on your fridge. Notes that say things like, "buy more cat butts." Cute, but useless.

My sister-in-law gave me a fake rock that has "meow" printed on it in gold foil. It has a picture of a fish on it as well. How these two things complement each other, I don't know, but I now have a meow-fish rock. Ok, what am I to do with it?

Honestly, any ideas? It's not a bank nor is it a key holder. It's just a fake rock. I was at a loss on what to do with it so I cut a hole in the top and stuck a sword-shaped letter opener in it. Now I have King Arthur's Excalibur sword–in-the-stone sitting on my dresser only it says "meow" on it (along with a picture of a fish).

I have many cat figurines; I get cat photos in my emails and posted to my Facebook wall. I am inundated with cat toys that Kolby won't play with.

The only really useful cat items I get are bags of food that kind folks like to give me. Keep those coming folks. True fact: on the day I was writing this story (while at work, please don't say anything to my boss), I got home to find two huge bags of food left on my landing by a donor or donors unknown.

On this occasion, I was re-gifted an audio-animatronic feline (as Disney Imagineers would proclaim). Or, as most would call it, a robot cat. It had originally been purchased to supply companionship for an elderly woman but, unfortunately, she never had the chance to enjoy its company so it sat in a box in a spare room for many years....until it came to live with me.

This mechanical cat is really quite the engineering marvel. If Walt Disney had made it past 1965 (darn those cigarettes!), he would indeed be amazed to see the type of robotic creatures we can buy at any toy store or discount center for a few bucks. I am amazed as well. Robotic people will be available shortly for just $19.95. You will probably find them in the electronics aisle by the toilets that flush themselves (or maybe even ON the toilets if any of the stock boys are merry pranksters).

This life-sized, all-white cat can do the following: meow, purr, blink, hiss, twitch an ear, nod, stick out a tiny pink tongue, swish its tail and explain the theory of relativity. It is so life-like that it is off-putting and somewhat creepy. Holding it, I felt a bit like Dr. Frankenstein when his creature uttered its first "Argggh!"

So I was given a pretty yellow gift bag with wads of tissue paper billowing over the top like tiny clouds. As I let the cat out of the bag (rim-shot), she hissed at me through the courtesy of 4 AA batteries. Then she closed her eyes and purred. I was immediately in love. I named her Whitey (fitting, though hardly original). One of these days, when I get the courage, I am going to take her to my vet and see how they react when I explain that Whitey doesn't seem to be eating and I am afraid she might become anorexic. That would be funny! I'll let you know how it goes and whether they call the cops.

We had quite a bit of fun with Whitey the night of our gift exchange, but I knew a real challenge was to come. What would Kolby do when I took her home? Based upon his reaction to Blackie, I could see this ending in gunplay. But, then again, would he know that Whitey wasn't real? I thought it would be interesting to see his historic meeting with that cat that never was. In the morning, I fed Kolby as usual and watched him go through his normal routine. A little poo, a little play, a little rub against my leg. Then he was off to nap. I waited until he was on his way upstairs and took Whitey out of the bag. Placing her on the floor in the middle of the living room, I flipped her switch on and called for Kolby to come downstairs. I heard him clumping down the stairs.

As he came around the corner into the living room, he saw Whitey for the first time. He stopped and looked at her closely. His tail went to a soft DEFCON 1, slightly puffed, but he remained calm. He meowed quietly and took several hesitant steps toward her. Whitey sat there unmoving.

As Kolby reached Whitey, her motion sensors kicked in. She blinked and bobbed her head. Kolby was within a few inches now and he slowly leaned in to smell her cheeks, his nose bobbing gently against her fur. This is where a cat's scent glands are located. This is why they rub against you with their cheeks. They plant their scent on you and mark their territory so other cats may know you are no longer the orphaned rag-a-muffin you once were. Kolby detected no scent.

He then turned to her feet. Surely they could give some account of her movements. Could he detect the hint of grass, dirt,

{ Kolby has chosen food over females his entire life.
What can you do? }

leaves, or litter-box? Nothing there either. He walked away from her a few paces to digest this information, then went back to sniff that hallowed sanctum that all animals check out sooner or later: the naughty bits. However, Whitey was sitting down and even though Kolby prodded her with a paw, she demurely refused to stand.

By now, Kolby was coming to the conclusion that there wasn't much to be concerned about. This chick wasn't real. She didn't smell right. He started to purr and, mayhaps by chance, Whitey started to purr too. There they sat, purring loudly at each other.

Kolby went behind her and lay down. He reached out a paw and batted at her tail. The tail swished angrily away from him. He grabbed at it with both paws and pulled it toward him. At this affront to her sovereignty, Whitey hissed loudly and meowed. Kolby dropped the tail and bolted upright. His eyes were big as saucers and he looked around the room for the source of this cat-like sound. Nothing. Whitey hissed again and Kolby sat transfixed. This thing looked real and sounded real and while he was 99.9% sure it was simply smoke and mirrors, it was still very confusing.

In the next few days, on occasion, Kolby would pad-foot over to where Whitey sat under the end table in the living room. If Whitey was turned on (not in THAT way, of course), she would meow and Kolby would give her a sniff. Mostly he was just satisfying himself that his first assessment was accurate. There was no truth behind this white lie. It was all fluff and no substance.

Since the time of Christ, there have been false messiahs who have preyed on the most vulnerable among us. They may look the part, they may sound like they know what they're talking about and on the surface their ideas may sound reasonable, but when all is said and done, it is fluff and no substance. Jesus specifically warned us about such people. Wolves dressed as sheep, he called them. They have no concern for anything but themselves and will enter the fold simply to rend and tear the flock while making a quick buck in the process.

In the intervening years since this warning was given, many have been deceived and have fallen victim to lies and half-truths spun in plausible sounding ways. Many have died as a result. Do you think all the Kool-Aid drinkers in Jonestown ever felt they were on the wrong path? Nope. Up until the time the cyanide killed them, they were absolutely convinced that they were on the path to heaven when all along it was the road to destruction.

How about those poor misguided "Heaven's Gate" people? They died in their beds waiting to be transported by UFO to a much better place than this. The Mothership never came for them; just the undertaker.

David Koresh and Charles Manson cast a spell on their

followers that was as close to devil possession as I have ever seen. Evil has rarely been so fully personified, yet they were seen as messiahs by both sets of their followers. Their preaching, rather than inspiring a person to reach lofty heights and draw closer to the perfection of the Father, led only to murder and death. I can go on with example after example in a shameful litany of dead and dying, all having perished with a prayer on their lips and a lie in their hearts. The question is why, for cryin' out loud, are so many people fooled by this garbage?

The answer to this question is profoundly simple: they could not discern the truth. If you know the true, you will not be fooled by the false.

Counterfeiting is a huge problem worldwide. In 2012, the Secret Service seized $261,000,000 in phony bills in the US alone. While this represents only a pittance of the cash passed around the USA on any one day, it is still a significant hit to the economy as these bills have no value. Once found, they are destroyed and the poor sap holding them is out the cash. You don't get reimbursed for passing a fake buck even if it was completely innocent on your part, which is often the case. Odds are, at some point, you may have passed a counterfeit bill without realizing it (I know I did, but that's another story for another time). Banks, businesses and institutions like the post office are constantly on guard against accepting look-alike cash. Employees are trained in the art of spotting fakes.

There's the key word: "trained." Bank employees would be no better than you or I at spotting a bogus bill if they did not receive training from an expert. I know little about diamonds. I know they were once lumps of charcoal suitable for cooking a juicy burger. I know they are now pretty and sparkly and, according to Marilyn Monroe, they are a girl's best friend, but you could sell me a chunk of glass from an old pop bottle and, if it were cut right, I would not know the difference. I could lose a bunch of money speculating in the diamond market unless I spent a lot of time studying diamonds. Since this subject holds no interest for me, I won't be buying a truckload of gems any time soon. Plus, I don't have the money to dabble in diamonds anyway. To know true from false takes an effort on our part. It takes study.

This leads us to the real question. It is one that the human race has been asking since...well, forever. The Roman prefect, Pontius Pilate, asked this question of Jesus when he said, "What is truth?" Here's the answer to that very important query: "Thy word is truth." John 17:17 (KJV). The Bible is the word of God. It is the ultimate arbiter of truth.

Truth does not change. It is not a fashion that goes in and out of style like the platform shoes and bell-bottom jeans I wore in the 70s that seem to be making a comeback (a sure sign of the coming apocalypse). Situations may change. Ideas come and go. Ethics and morality may be revisited, but truth remains the same. It is a rock that we can build upon.

Too many people think they have a good handle on what the Bible is all about. There are a plethora of self-proclaimed Biblical scholars who, in actuality, know very little about the book. You'll hear them quoting non-existent verses they heard in some movie dialogue, or expounding at length on what the Bible says about a certain subject when in reality they are simply regurgitating some urban scriptural legend for which no correlation in scripture can be found. A classic example springs to mind in the oft misquoted verse, "money is the root of all evil." The Bible does not say this. It says, "The love of money is the root of all evil." Subtle difference, huge impact.

A majority of people have formulated concepts that are rooted in nothing more than their own preconceived notions. In short, they twist the Bible to justify their beliefs rather than study the Bible to learn what those beliefs should be. This is the broad path to destruction.

The Bible is a book that is not meant to be read; it is meant to be studied. It is a road map to your salvation and must be understood in its entirety. Although the book is full of poetry, history, morality plays, scary, scary beasts and some really funny stories, it is not a book for a light afternoon of perusal.

If finding a path to the Father's throne room has any meaning to you, then you must study His Word. In it, you'll find everything you need to know to make it safely home.

The Bible is all about Jesus. His life and times are not contained in just the four Gospels. The entire Bible is about Him. The Old Testament points forward to his life and death, the New Testament points backward to the cross. It all revolves around Him. His fingerprints are all over this world from beginning to end; from creator to redeemer.

Jesus told us, "Search the scriptures, for in them you hope that you have eternal life, and they testify concerning Me", John 5:39 (ABPE). Notice His admonition is not, "Let someone else search the scriptures and then give you the gist of it." YOU must search the scriptures for YOURSELF.

In 1958, an oil exploration team searching in the Libyan Desert came across an almost perfectly preserved WWII era bomber lying uncovered in the sand. Painted on the nose of the plane was the name "Lady Be Good."

Upon checking records, it was discovered that the "Lady Be Good" had been part of a bombing raid in 1943. Launching from a site in Libya, the B-24D Liberator had crossed the Mediterranean to take part in a raid on Naples. It never returned. No one ever knew what happened to the plane and its nine man crew. It simply vanished. Fifteen years later, the plane's tragic end became known.

As found, the wreck was so perfectly preserved by the arid desert air that a thermos of tea found in the plane was still drinkable. The .50 caliber machine guns fired on the first pull of the trigger. The radio still broadcast.

Personal effects were still in the plane, untouched by the years. But the crew was gone. No sign of them was found at the site. It was like an eerie Twilight Zone episode. Subsequent searches turned up the bodies of all but one crewmember scattered along an invisible path in the sand.

The most important find was the diary kept by one of the crew. This diary documented the entire tale in great detail and allowed the world to finally know the full story of what happened. Flying back from the raid late at night, the plane overshot its landing beacon. Thinking they were still flying over the Mediterranean Sea, the crew flew deeper and deeper into the vast reaches of the great Libyan Desert. Finally, over four hundred miles inland, they ran out of fuel.

The crew bailed out expecting to land in the water. Instead they hit the beach, literally. Almost all the crew survived and was able to reunite as a team about sixteen miles north of where the plane came to rest. As they took stock of the supplies they had on hand, they found one of them was carrying a military issued map of desert roadways, camps and other landmarks of civilization. Studying the map, they decided that walking northwest was their best way to survive and reach help. So they set off thinking the coastline could not be far.

During the day, they baked in the sun at temperatures of 130F. At night they froze in their light uniforms. Always they kept going, following the only map they had. On and on they marched, one day, two days, five days, eight days. One by one they began to drop, giving in to the inevitable and finding sweet release in death. Finally, only one man was left. Incredibly, this man managed to walk over 110 miles in the desert. Alone, without water or food, he kept putting one foot in front of the other until he, too, lay down and let go.

It's an epic tale of valor and courage. It is also a tragic tale of futility. You see, the map they were following was hopelessly outdated. It was wrong. They spent their strength; they put their faith in a map that led them in the wrong direction. If only they had had a reliable map, they could have walked to the south. Walking south would have led them to their plane and its supply of food and water. Further south, the oasis of Wadhi Zighen with its life-giving water lay within walking distance. Instead they walked north because the map said to. They died because the path they were on was the wrong one. According to the map, it looked like the right thing to do but it led to death.

"There is a path before each person that seems right, but it ends in death." Proverbs 16:25 (NLT). The Bible is God's road map to us. It is our personal GPS, God's Plan of Salvation. Is it difficult to fathom at times? Sure is. Is it impossible to know and understand? Not at all. "Certainly the sovereign Lord does nothing without first revealing his plan to his servants the prophets." Amos 3:7 (NET). But it will take more effort on your part than a casual perusal. You won't pass the oral exam by reciting the CliffsNotes on this book. You must study this map. Closely, carefully, daily.

Kolby wasn't fooled by Whitey. He knew what the true looked like and even though the false was compelling at first, in the end, it didn't pass the smell test.

CHAPTER NINE:
Super Duper Pooper Scooper

Whoever conceals their sins does not prosper, but the one who confesses and renounces them finds mercy.
- Proverbs 28:13 (NIV)

At this time in our nation's history, it seems we as a populace are pretty much split right down the middle politically with each of the two parties sharing the vote equally. That's why we have such close hard-fought elections with our candidates fighting like cats and dogs.

Speaking of cats and dogs, Americans are pretty much split right down the middle on their pets too. Cats and dogs are by far the most popular pets in the USA and ownership is right at 50/50. Cats have a slight edge in sheer numbers but dogs take the lead among households who own a pet.

Personally, I like both. I like dogs because they have the unique ability to make us feel as if we are the most important person who ever existed in the entire universe. They hang on our every word and slavishly follow our every move. Being around a dog gives you a wonderfully inflated sense of self esteem.

My neighbors have a dog named Bogart. He is a black lab, and I've known him over the back fence since he was a puppy. He's a wonderful dog. He does not bark unless there is a need. If Bogart is barking late at night, you can be sure something's up that needs attention. He is always happy and friendly. He never growls or offers his fangs. I'm not sure he knows how.

In the mornings when I leave for work, if Bogart is outside, the minute he sees me he runs to the fence by the garage and waits for me to come over and say hello. On mornings I am running late and cannot do more than give him a shout out, he hangs his head in sorrow. But he's over it in a minute and away he goes for some other great adventure. At night when I get home, there is no better way to rid oneself of a lackluster work day than to visit Bogart for a minute. He will be at the fence waiting:

Me: "Hi, Bogart."

Bogart, wiggling with excitement: *"That's MY name! He said my name!"*

"Have you been a good boy today?"

"Have I been a good boy?" Jump, jump. *"Yes."* Jump, jump, *"I have!"* Jump, jump.

"What did you do today?"

"What did I do? What did I do? Let me see…I barked at a rabbit; I dug a few new holes in the flower bed and then I napped. After that, I just waited for you to get home and now here you are and everything is just great and…hey! Where are you going?"

"I'll see you tomorrow Bogart."

"Wait! I thought you were staying forever. You're really leaving? Ok, then; see you tomorrow?"

Cats, on the other hand, have a way of making us feel as if we have failed them in some manner. They are like a good Jewish mother. We don't know how we failed, or where we failed, we only know we failed them. Kolby will often give me that look in

106

the morning as I am ready to leave:

Me: "What?"

Kolby: *"Nothing, I was just wondering if that's all the breakfast I'm getting?"*

"That was plenty. You didn't even eat it all"

"Meh, I've had better. It was a little dry."

"You didn't complain when you ate a whole bowl of the same thing yesterday. Anyway, I'll be home at noon."

"I'll be here. Where else would I be but waiting all alone in this big house."

"You can nap in the sun. You like to nap."

"Yes, yes, with your friends, go. Have fun. Don't worry about me. I'll nap in the sun. I should care if I get skin cancer? On my deathbed, maybe you'll be sorry."

"Whatever."

The main reason I chose to live with a cat rather than a dog pertains to their bathroom issues. Let's face facts folks, dogs are slobs. Bogart's yard is a mess. The evidences of his travels around the yard are everywhere, and one must step lightly and with great care so as not to hit one of his homemade land mines. And he is nonplussed by the negative attention his actions receive. He has no shame. Bogart will leave something on the lawn, turn and look you right in the eye and claim, *"It was like that when I got here."*

Cats are demur and do not like to call attention to the fact they are in need of the litter box. They require no special training either. Just show them to the box, and they can take it from there. I purchased many of the supplies needed to care for a cat before I had gotten one and when Kolby selected me at the shelter I had not taken size into account. He is larger than the average housecat by quite a bit, and the box I bought was too small to accommodate him. The bomb bay doors were never on target and, as a result, the payload was often delivered over the edge of his box. Then he would use his front paws to scoop the litter from the box onto the floor to cover his transgression.

I fixed this easily enough by getting him a huge litter box with a square footage roughly the size of Rhode Island (Rhode Islanders, please do not think for a minute that I am comparing your state to a cat's litter box. I have never been to Rhode Island but have heard many good things about it, none of which currently come to mind. But I sincerely hope to visit one day and sample all of the things that make your state the great place it is said to be by people who no longer live there).

One of the least glamorous aspects of the exciting high-stakes world of International Pet Ownership is the need to perform a ritual I call "The Cleansing of the Litter Box." This is best done daily but in a pinch can be stretched out to intervals of three days. I do not recommend going longer than four (I did that once and poor Kolby had his box so full It was like a New Orleans cemetery with one body stacked on top of another).

It is a distasteful job to be sure, but I have found that role playing is a good way to make the whole experience more palatable. Since I have long been a fan of Robert Louis Stevenson's "Treasure Island", I play the role of the one-legged, seafaring scalawag, Long John Silver, while Kolby does an admirable job as Jim Hawkins or, if need be, Blind Pew.

Me (in my best pirate voice): "Aye, matey. Be ye ready to find Flint's treasure?"
Kolby: *"Me-arrrr!"*

Then with scoop in hand, we go on a jolly treasure hunt. When we are finished, we have a whole bag of gold and silver doubloons (just don't try spending them at Wal-Mart).

One day I was sitting on the floor cleaning the box when it struck me. My whole life is one big litter box and God is constantly cleaning up my messes.

Sin is a word we rarely use anymore. It is an archaic term that is in danger of passing from our nomenclature because to our modern ears it sounds puritanical and judgmental. We don't want to label anyone a "sinner" as we may hurt their feelings or insult them. We like softer words or phrases such as, "I made a mistake." The politician caught with his hand in the cookie jar has not broken the commandment "Thou shalt not steal" and committed a sin. They just made a mistake. The TV commercial that tells you their product is guaranteed not to "rip, rattle or bag at the knees" when it fact it does all three of those things simultaneously, has not lied to you; they just exercised some creative salesmanship. The coach who's mantra is "winning is everything" and then breaks the rules to be sure his team wins is not labeled a "cheater." He is just "passionate." Sin ain't what it used to be.

But here let me confess before God and my country, I am a sinner. Sin, as defined in the scriptures, is the transgression of God's law. That's what I do. While outwardly I may appear to you to be the very epitome of an urbane, handsome and witty gentleman (why, thank you!), inwardly it's a far different story. I have too much pride which, as the scripture opines, is one of the worst sins. I might even go so far as to say I am proud of my pride. I anger easily and smolder long. There are a bunch of people I don't like and one whole state I've written off entirely (no, it is not Rhode Island. I have nothing against Rhode Island, and I am sorry I ever brought them up. I won't tell you which state but they know).

"Big Deal," you say. "So you don't like a few loudmouths. It's not like you ever murdered somebody." True, except for the fact that Jesus said if you hate your brother you have killed your brother. If that's the case then I have a whole lot of notches on my gun.

I constantly doubt God and can get depressed and anxious over life's details. In short, I am just like the rest of you. As scripture tells us, "All have sinned and come short of the glory of God". And we, like Kolby, are very good at covering up our transgressions. Rather than confess our sins to God and finding mercy, we just keep burying them in the sand until the litter box is full to overflowing.

So every day, the committed Christian should be on their

knees in prayer asking forgiveness for the areas we have failed Him and asking for the faith and power to become the people God wants us to be. I must let God take away my pride so that He, in turn, can be proud of me.

There's a great story in the Bible found in Matthew 8:1-3 about a leper who sought healing at the feet of Jesus.

Leprosy was a terrible scourge and one of the most feared diseases in the time of Christ. There was no cure. There was no treatment. Once you contracted leprosy, that was pretty much it. You just waited to die. During that time, the disease ravaged your body. Fingers and toes, ears and nose all just disappeared. Skin turned scaly and rough. Muscles atrophied and blindness was a common side effect. By the time the disease had run its course, what had once been a human being was now just a twisted lump of rotting flesh. Since the disease is not terminal (most often you died as a result of complications from the disease rather than the disease itself), you spent many years in the process of dying. During this period of living death, you were ostracized from your community, your friends, your family and most importantly, as they believed, from God.

The Jews called leprosy, "The finger of God." This reflected their belief that the disease was a judgment God hit you with directly because of the great sin that existed in your life. This belief was wrongly held but quite common. Even Christ's disciples held this twisted view of God the Father. They thought that God had put a visible mark upon you to differentiate you from other lesser sinners. You were the worst of a bad lot. You also had no hope of redemption. No hope of an afterlife. No hope of salvation. You were toast.

When we understand this mindset, we can see the great courage and faith it took for the leper to approach Jesus in the first place. If Jesus was indeed, as some were calling Him, the Son of God, then this leper was asking the very God who had given him the disease in the first place to now heal him of it. This, in case you've ever wondered, is the definition of irony.

110

So here a leper and a sinner lies in the dust at the Master's feet. He has barely summoned the courage to make such a bold request: "Lord, if you want to, you can make me whole." WWJD?

At this point, Jesus has several options. He can send the man away letting him die from his sinful disease. After all, the guy probably deserved it. He can call the cops because what the man had done was illegal. By law, a leper could not come in proximity to someone healthy. He could ignore the leper and move on to another town, leaving the problem for someone else to deal with. Or He could take this opportunity to show the world what God was really like.

The request was, "Lord if you want to, you can make me whole." As Jesus gazed down at the man, His heart was moved with compassion. He saw this man as he had been, what he had become, and what he could be once again and He answered simply, "I want to." All of God's love is summed up in those three words. His mission, His purpose and His passion are defined in those three words.

Then Jesus did the unthinkable. He did that which was forbidden by law. He reached out and touched the man. He actually put His hands right on those scaly, rotting lumps that passed for flesh, and he healed him. From head to toe, the man was suddenly clean and free from the disease.

If you have read any of the other recorded events when Jesus exercised His healing power, there are only a few instances that mention Him touching someone during the healing process. One instance was in a clinical fashion when He made a mud compound used to anoint a blind man's eyes. Most often He simply spoke, and it was done. But this time He made a special point to touch the man. It was an intimate human gesture designed to show the leper he was loved and accepted. When no one else wanted to be around him, God would draw near. When no one else would touch him, God would stoop to put His hands on him. When everyone else told him he was getting what he deserved, Jesus was showing him the value heaven put upon one undeserving sinner.

These three short verses in the book of Matthew lay out the entire plan of salvation. When sin entered this world, it became one vast leper colony. It was cut off from the courts of heaven and quarantined from the rest of God's creation. For the transgression of God's Law there was no cure, no treatment and no hope. But God had a plan. His own son would bear the penalty and die the death we deserve. Now, we lepers can come to Jesus and cast ourselves at his feet saying, "Lord if you want to, you can make me whole." He will reply, "I want to."

"If we confess our sins, He is faithful and just to forgive us our sins and to cleanse us from all unrighteousness." First John 1:9 (KJV). We need to stop burying our sins and acting like they don't exist or don't matter. Soon that litter box will no longer be able to cover up what's underneath the surface. Although I wish he could, Kolby cannot clean his own litter box. All he can do is keep adding to it. Neither can we clear up the sin in our life. Left to ourselves, we can only keep on adding to them.

God has a Super Duper Pooper Scooper. Just say the word and He can scoop out all of those sins and put them in the trash where they belong leaving your life clean and fresh and ready for a new day.

Chapter Ten:

The Good, the Bad, and the Ugly

And if you say that someone is worthless, you will be in danger of the fires of hell.
- Matthew 5:22 (CEV)

We human beings must live in accordance with certain immutable laws of the universe. Science, through experimentation and observation, has managed to detail some of these laws. Here are three.

Immutable law number one states: If you put ten socks in the dryer, you will get only nine back. This law is known as the "Odd/Even Devaluation Equation." In short it states that no matter how many pairs of socks go in the dryer, one sock will always come up missing. It does no good to try and circumvent this law by putting five pairs of good socks and a single old ratty one in the dryer. The law recognizes this attempt to deceive and for punishment will take away two good socks leaving you with two old maids. It will also spit out the old ratty sock just to mock you.

Many researchers believe this law came into effect at the same time hot-air tumble dryers were introduced but this is not true. Our ancient ancestors had the same problem. They would take their socks to the river to wash by dipping them in the water and then slapping them against a rock. The wash cycle went: dip, slap, dip, slap, dip, slap, slap, repeat.

Let's assume for argument's sake that they were washing four socks. As the echo of the last slap faded, they would discover they now held only three. This resulted in very bad tempers, and yet another raid against a neighboring tribe to obtain more socks.

Immutable law number two says: If you have to wee-wee very, very badly, some article of clothing will automatically malfunction causing you an uncomfortable delay. Usually this is the zipper that has somehow managed to get the pull tab lodged in the folds of material. Then you have to dig through the medicine cabinet to find something like a nail file or the wife's toothbrush to poke in there and get it loose. Once an appropriate tool has been located, you must then free the tab while hopping from one foot to the other, hoping you make it in time.

Immutable law number three states: Your kitchen will dirty itself overnight. Say you leave several dirty dishes in the sink because you don't want to empty the dishwasher tonight as you are too tired. When you get up in the morning, you will now find a whole pile of dirty dishes scattered on the counter and have no idea how they got there. Your cupboards will be empty of plates and glasses. Some of the dishes on the counter you won't recognize as yours. One morning I found a colander in the sink. I didn't even know I owned a colander.

The other night I was in the kitchen cleaning up the mess it had done to itself, when the outside motion-activated light came on. Usually this means either Blackie is coming up the steps for dinner or that a hoard of undead zombies is lurching toward the house with the intention of using my brain as a cheese ball. Fortunately in this case, it was Blackie.

I looked out the window and sure enough there was

Blackie heading up the steps. I looked to his bowl to be sure he had food and did a double take in disbelief. There was another Blackie with his head buried in the food bowl! I closed my eyes and opened them again. Nope. I was not seeing things. There were two black cats out on the landing.

Two Blackies! But which one was which? As my eyes adjusted to the dim light, I saw that my Blackie was on the steps, and another Blackie was the one with his head in the bowl. (I named them "Classic" Blackie and "New" Blackie in homage to the popular soft drink. I thought about calling them "original recipe" Blackie and "extra crispy" Blackie but that brought up an unpleasant image.)

I saw that while Classic Blackie is solid black, New Blackie has a streak of white across his front paws, and he was not in the best condition. He was thin, and his fur was dirty and unkempt. He looked like he just hopped off a freight train down at the yard, and indeed that could have been the case as we live only a few blocks from a switch yard. He certainly needed the food.

Classic Blackie stood back and assessed the situation quietly. He was not about to give up his territory without a fight, but he was not yet ready to light that candle. New Blackie, on the other hand, was ready to rumble.

If you have ever heard a cat fight, you know that the noise is usually much worse than the actual fight. It begins at a low volume and progresses to an ear-splitting yowling, and that was just the direction this confrontation was heading. Kolby, who to this point had been completely unaware that he now had two cats to contend with, ran into the kitchen to see what was happening. I, for my part, could not let this escalate into a physical confrontation between the two cats, so I opened the door with the intention of shooing off at least one of the Blackies until I could figure out how to deal with the situation.

It was then Kolby saw them both. He immediately went to DEFCON 5. He looked like a porcupine with the mumps. If he puffed himself any further, I think he would have floated up to bump gently against the ceiling.

One of my all-time favorite films is the 1966 Classic Italian western, "The Good, The Bad, and the Ugly." I saw that when I was 14 (and many times since) and as a teenage boy you cannot forget the impact that such a film has. Especially the groundbreaking soundtrack by composer Ennio Morricone; "Ah-EE-Ah-EE-Ah, Wah, Wah, Wah!"

Right at that moment I was re-living the climactic final scene where the three title characters stare each other down before the final big shootout. There was the Good (Classic Blackie), the Bad (Kolby) and the Ugly (New Blackie).

They warily eyed one another. Kolby paced and growled while New Blackie hissed and yowled. Classic Blackie gave them both the steely-eyed Clint Eastwood squint. I let them go on for a few minutes (while I laughed) and then decided I would break it up. I stepped to the door and yelled "Boo!" as loud as I could. All three took off. Kolby went upstairs under the bed, while both Blackies ran in different directions down the block.

As much as I would like to see peace among the three, I cannot force them to like each other. They will have to work that out for themselves. I do know that until they do, there will be unhappy consequences for all three. Kolby's life has become very agitated. Running to the door at any little sound. Sleeping lightly and flinching at shadows. He is no longer at peace in his own house. The two Blackies are in danger of having nothing to eat or drink. They both may choose to stay away from the house for fear they would meet and heaven forbid that happen. The old saw of cutting off your nose to spite your face comes to mind.

Every day, we meet people we don't like. People who are selfish. People who are self-absorbed. People who think more highly of themselves than they should. People who dismiss you as unworthy of their attention. One of my personal peeves is the person who shakes your hand, but is too important or busy to look at you while they do it. They give you a weak couple of shakes while talking or looking at something or someone else. A political candidate did that to me once. Needless to say, he did not get my vote.

People tailgate us while we're driving; they cut ahead of us in line after we have waited patiently for what seems like hours. They would cheerfully cheat us out of our money, and they feel no remorse for taking our items for their own. They tell lies that hurt us. Their actions cause us problems. Their words humiliate. In worse cases, they hurt us physically, leaving deep, emotional scars.

We have good *reason* to dislike such people. However, the truth is we have no *right* to dislike such people. Here's why. We have done far worse to God, and he has forgiven us. We killed his son. We caused discord in Heaven. We misrepresent his character. We disregard His laws. We have willingly followed other gods such as fame and wealth. Yet, while we were still His enemies, He came to seek and save the lost.

Don't think for a minute that I am trying to lecture you from some position of great moral superiority. I am the last person to give anyone a talk on loving your neighbor. I am Italian and everything that implies. I have a temper I got from my father. I don't suffer fools well. While my good Christian mother was teaching me I must love and forgive, my father was telling me that in a street fight there are no rules. I've struggled with this dichotomy my whole life.

Fact is we will get angry with others and often we will have good cause. But that anger cannot be allowed to fester. The Bible tells us to deal with it before the sun goes down. In other words, if at all possible, before the day is over, let it go.

When we get angry with someone and hold on to that anger, we want nothing more to do with them. To us they are already dead. We have murdered them in our hearts. We have dismissed them as someone not worthy of our friendship or love. In so doing, we have dismissed them as someone unworthy of salvation. At one time, we may have been the conduit through which God draws them to Himself. Not now, that opportunity has passed.

In the passages of the Bible, people can find much to argue about. We parse every phrase for hidden meaning and come up with a hundred different (and wrong) interpretations. But the words spoken by Jesus in Matthew chapter five are as plain as any ever put to paper. If we do not learn to forgive, we will not be forgiven. Let's extrapolate that thought to its' logical conclusion. If we are not forgiven, we will not have a place in heaven. No amount of good works, no surfeit of biblical knowledge, not even martyrdom will compensate for an unforgiving nature. We will have no place at the banquet table because we do not belong.

Jesus told a story about a servant who owed his king a fortune. It was more money than he could earn in several lifetimes. He could never repay that debt. So he threw himself on the king's mercy. The king forgave him the entire amount. Rather than be happy, this ungrateful servant went out and found a guy who owed him the equivalent of about $10 and tried to beat it out of him. Of course when the king heard about this, he hauled the servant back in and sold him, his family and all their possessions to pay the debt.

God has forgiven us a debt we could never pay. We have

no right to beat up each other over the little things. Kolby has no right to complain that other cats are invading his territory. It's not his territory. I own that house. I pay the mortgage. I pay for heat, lights, water and insurance. He lives there because I love him, and it pleases me to have him as a friend. The two Blackies have no right to fight each other over the food I provide. I go to the store and buy it. I carry it to the car. I open the bag and put it in the food bowl. Without my providence, they go hungry.

God sends the Good News of salvation to all. We have no right to decide who is worthy and who is unworthy to receive it.

I would love to stay and lecture some more but right now I have to go to the store and see if I can find three cat-size cowboy hats. In case there's another confrontation, I want them to look the part. I'll take a video if I can. "Ah-EE-Ah-EE-Ah! Wah, Wah, Wah!"

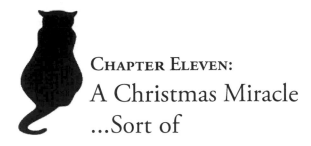

CHAPTER ELEVEN

A Christmas Miracle ...Sort of

And I am certain that God, who began the good work within you, will continue his work until it is finally finished on the day when Christ Jesus returns.
\- Philippians 1:6 (NLT)

I am not a wealthy man as some would count wealth. The excesses of the rich and richer are not my playground.

At a restaurant in Vegas, a person can order a burger and fries at the paltry price of $5,000.00. Add a milkshake for $500.00, and you've got the world's most expensive Happy Meal and it doesn't even come with a toy car.

If you're not hungry enough to do justice to a $5,000.00 burger, you may dine on a single truffle at a juke joint in New York for only $95,000.00. You read that correctly. Ninety-five grand for something a pig dug up with its nose. Again, it does not come with a toy car (although you'd think at that price they could toss in a real car).

By extrapolating (I love that word) my current monthly food fund allotment, I have determined it would take me roughly twenty-nine years to spend $95,000.00 on food, and that includes feeding Kolby! For me, that truffle-munching dining experience could be summed up as ten minutes of pleasure followed by twenty-nine years of famine, accompanied each and every day by loud, angry protestations from one very annoyed cat.

While I'll never wolf down an expensive truffle or guzzle a $500 milkshake, I still consider myself a rich man where it counts the most because the Lord has blessed me abundantly with friends.

Social media has caused us to water down the meaning of the word friends. While Facebook and other apps are great ways to network, we often add friends based upon their friendship with someone else we know. They then add us as friends in return because it is insulting to NOT be added as a friend when you have afforded them that privilege and pretty soon we have a whole bunch of "friends" we really don't know other than through a selfie they have posted of themselves. Usually these selfies are meant to be comical in some way. Usually they are not and make us wonder just exactly where civilization is headed these days. Why, in my day, we sat still for a photo and showed some respect! Erect posture and a slight smile were all we needed to make a good photo! Well, it seems I've gotten off topic a tad. So when I say friends, I mean it in the old fashioned sense. Tried and true people I personally know and love. People who know me well and still manage to grit their teeth and like me. People I would trust with my life and everything I own.

These friends exist in two separate worlds. There are those friends within my church family and those friends of mine without a particular church affiliation (I affectionately call them Philistines). I have known my "outside" circle of friends (the Philistines) for nearly 40 years. We met around the medium of music and playing it. Most of them are excellent musicians and the ones who don't play are excellent listeners.

One thing that binds us together as friends is the fact we never do anything today that cannot be put off till tomorrow or next month if need be. In our way of thinking, procrastination is a virtue. This explains why our annual Christmas get-togethers are never at Christmas.

At one time, we managed to get together pretty close to December 25, but lately we keep celebrating further and further from the actual Christmas date.

This year, Christmas, for us, came on March 10th. I predict in a matter of a few years, we will be celebrating a combination Christmas/July Fourth holiday where we tie bottle rockets to the tree and see how far up it travels before it bursts into flame. Silent night indeed.

Our first Christmases were marked by lavish gift giving such as pricey burgers and spendy truffles. Then, we got older and figured it was just too much work to buy each other things we could easily afford to buy ourselves or already had. So we decided to give items that we found around the house or lying out in the yard. These items we dress up in a nice bow and pass on to one another instead of putting them in the landfill where they belong.

Witness the wonderful gifts I received this year alone. From friends Lee and Yvonne, I got an old pair of rubber Wellington-style boots that had been found in an alley next to a house in New Ulm, Minnesota. The givers had graciously hand-marked them as to which one went on the left or right foot. This saves me quite a bit of time when putting them on. Along with that, they also gave me a pair of used coveralls that they either could not, or would not, reveal the source of. Frankly, I'm not sure I care to know where they got them.

Among other items, my friends Dan and Bettie gave me a CD of Pat Boone, singing heavy metal rock songs such as "Smoke on the Water." I am not making this up. The album is titled *Pat Boone, No More Mr. Nice Guy* and features a photo of Pat sitting awkwardly on a custom chopper motorcycle, a mixed message if ever there was one (at least he wasn't sitting in one of those walk-in tubs he's been advertising lately). I made out like a bandit alright. What a haul.

But one of these couples made a mistake in their gift-a-palooza giving and presented Kolby and me with an item of great value. I'm sure they did not intend it to turn out this way, but they gave us a Christmas miracle...sort of.

Now that Kolby lives with me, he has been included in the gifting process and usually gets gifts on a par with the rest of us. This may be a bag of opened cat food or a figurine of a large lazy cat that is meant to point out the obvious fact that Kolby is a large lazy cat (he gets the joke, but he sees no humor in the comparison).

For Kolby this year, Dan and Bettie brought him one of those cat toys where a spinning wire arm goes around in an erratic circular motion underneath a skirt of yellow fabric. The movement of the arm is impossible to predict. This herky-jerky movement fascinates a cat and as the commercials show, drives them insane trying to catch the "mouse."

There is no doubt that Marley was dead. This must be distinctly understood, or nothing wonderful can come of the story I am going to relate. Wait a minute! How did I segue into *A Christmas Carol* by Charles Dickens? Oh, now I see it. Let me try that again....

There is no doubt that Kolby does not play with toys. This must be distinctly understood, or nothing wonderful can come of the story I am going to relate. Kolby has never been a playful cat. I've bought him many toys, and they all go begging in the corner. Little balls with bells in them – ho-hum. Bouncy spring-loaded mice to bat at – thank you, no. Kitty-size fishing rods with feathers at the end of the line – you've got to be kidding. He does not play with any of this type of manufactured toy.

Even as we were setting up Kolby's new toy, I was telling the group not to be disappointed if he paid no attention to it. He may give it a cursory glance, but they should not expect any actual interest on his part. We finished the assembly process, put the toy on the floor and turned it on. It was then the miracle occurred.

Kolby ran to the toy. He sat down by it and watched with unwavering concentration. He reached out a hesitant paw to touch the arm as it flew past. Much like a deer in the headlights, he could not look away.

He hunkered down in the stereotypical hunting cat pose; body pressed to the floor and tail twitching ever so slightly behind him. His eyes darted around the ring as the arm flailed left and right. Then he pounced. Or tried to. His pouncing skills leave much to be desired. He failed to catch the arm, and as it swept around toward him he jumped back out of its path. He pounced once more, missed, and got slapped in the face as the arm swung past. He sat there for a good five minutes watching and pouncing and batting and playing!

I finally went over and turned it off to break the spell he was under and give him a chance to collect himself. When the arm stopped, he looked at me and meowed.

Kolby: *"Turn it on, turn it on!"*
Me: "Kitty, calm down. This much excitement is not good for your heart."
"Turn it back on, man, or I'll bite you good!"
"Hey, easy, easy. I'll turn it on. There, it's back on, we good? We cool man?"
"Yeah, we cool, now back off!"

It was like a drug for Kolby. In the middle of the night, he left the bed to go downstairs and sit next to it even though there was no way I was going to start it up at four in the morning.

The next day his interest hadn't waned. His itinerary that morning was: breakfast, a quick check out the door to make sure his nemesis, Blackie, wasn't around, and then into the living room to play with his new toy.

True to form, however, in the days that followed, he figured out a way to play with the toy that required little effort on his part. Instead of batting at the arm as it flew past him, he lay with one paw under the fabric. Then, much the same as Mohammed with the mountain, he waits for the arm to come to him. Still, his interest shows no sign of abating and I call that a Christmas miracle.

When we think of miracles, we conjure up images of spectacular supernatural events. We don't want ambiguous, was-it-or-wasn't-it type miracles. We want in-your-face, no-doubt-about-it miracles. We like our miracles to be on a grand scale.

We envision the Red Sea sweeping back upon itself opening a dry land channel for the fleeing Israelites or Jesus standing calmly in the back of the boat telling the storm to take it down a notch. We think of fish vomiting out prophets, bread falling from the sky, men walking on water, Elijah ascending to heaven in a chariot of fire. Now those are miracles you can sink your teeth into! And of course, there's the mother of all great miracles: raising the dead.

The Israelites had seen many miracles in their day. While they were captives in Egypt, God rescued them with ten miraculous events. The giving of the Law at Mt. Sinai was accompanied by signs and wonders. They were guided in their journey by a supernatural cloud of smoke by day and a pillar of fire at night.

Then Jesus shows up, walking among them, healing the sick and lame. He fed the 5,000 with a few fish and several pieces of flat bread. In spite of all this, they were always seeking after a sign that He was who He claimed to be: the Messiah. Even though they had seen so many wonders before, they still needed just one more to believe. It finally reached the point that Jesus, in response to yet another request for Him to prove Himself by healing someone, said, "Will you never believe in me unless you see miraculous signs and wonders?" John 4:48 (NLT).

Today, we have much in common with Israel of old. We are still seeking that miraculous sign to confirm our belief. Many flock to the faith healers. If the healer can get grandma to jump up out of that wheelchair, then Hallelujah! God does exist!

Crowds will line up to view the image of Jesus on a toasted cheese sandwich. Others will pay good money to own it. If the statue is crying tears of blood, somehow that makes us feel better about our eternal soul. If only God would just make his presence known in a tangible, visible way, then we'd know for sure we are on the right path.

Of course, miracles, signs, and wonders have always played a part in God's plan for our salvation, but there's an issue when we place too much emphasis upon them. Miracles cannot and do not change hearts. They may impress you. They certainly will get your attention, but they will not melt a cold, cold heart.

Jesus told the parable of the Rich Man and Lazarus. Interestingly, he gave a name to one of the characters in the story, Lazarus. This is something He normally did not do. At the end of the tale, He said that even if Lazarus came back from the dead, it would not be enough to convince others to believe in Him.

Not long after He told this story, He performed another miracle. From the dead, He raised a man named, you guessed it, Lazarus. Just as He predicted, this miracle meant nothing to those who would not believe. It changed them not one iota.

I have some good friends in my home church. They invited a friend of theirs over for dinner. This particular friend made no bones about the fact he had no belief in God. He seemed to take great pride in this. During the small talk leading up to dinner, they told him that their water heater had just broken down and needed fixing. Strangely, as dinner was about to start, this young man asked if he could say grace. He then proceeded to challenge God to prove His existence by fixing the water heater.

God is not our trained monkey. He is not our very own handy man. He does not need to prove Himself with an assortment of parlor tricks to give us the evidence we need to believe.

But think for a minute. What if God had accepted the challenge and fixed the water heater? Do you think for one minute it would have changed this young man's mindset? No. It would not.

Shock and awe does not change hearts. What does change hearts is the still small voice that you hear deep within you.

"And He said, go forth, and stand upon the mount before the Lord. And, behold, the Lord passed by, and a great and strong wind rent the mountains, and brake in pieces the rocks before the Lord; but the Lord was not in the wind: and after the wind an earthquake; but the Lord was not in the earthquake: And after the earthquake a fire; but the Lord was not in the fire: and after the fire a still small voice." 1 Kings 19:11-12 (KJV).

That's where you'll find the miracle. In that still small voice, God calls you to His side. He draws you with reason and love. He changes you from the inside out. It is a miraculous process. God could care less about fixing a water heater, but He'll give everything He has to fix you.

I know a young man who was baptized at the age of twelve. At thirteen, he took up smoking. At fifteen, he started doing drugs and drinking. By twenty, he was heavily involved in meth usage. At twenty-five, he was diagnosed with Hepatitis C.

By the time he was thirty, his body was shot. He tried to

stop smoking but could not. He tried to stop drinking but could not. He was arrested for DUI four times in the matter of a few years. His life spiraled out of control.

At thirty-three, he was injured in a construction accident. Over the next few years, he underwent a painful series of surgeries. They failed, and he received a 100% disability rating. He kept on drinking. He kept on smoking. Now he was hooked on prescription pain meds too. He was a dead man walking.

Through it all, he never stopped hearing that still small voice calling him back to the home he had left twenty years before. He tried to listen but the drugs, alcohol and tobacco threw up a barrier. They built a wall he could not climb.

Finally in desperation he threw himself on the floor one night and cried out to God to fix him. He got up off the floor and never smoked another cigarette. God had taken the addiction away. He threw out the drugs and poured the booze down the sink and never looked back.

Now, at forty, he lives in constant crippling pain. He knows that his body will never recover from the punishment it took in his younger years. He knows he is not looking at a long and active old age, but he is content and he told me, "For the first time in my life, I'm happy. I know whatever happens, the Lord has saved me, and that is all I need."

I know this story to be true for this young man is my nephew.

Every time we do not respond to someone in the way they deserve, but respond to them as Jesus would, that's a miracle. Believe me, with my nature, when I don't respond to a bad driver by flashing them a rude gesture, that's a miracle that God has wrought in my life.

When we show an interest in studying God's word, it's a miracle. When we desire to share the gospel with others, it's a miracle. When we forgive another's trespasses, it's a miracle that rivals the parting of the Red Sea. We ask for signs and wonders every day and never stop to consider that the greatest miracle God does is within our hearts.

Our Scripture verse tells us God has begun a good work within us, and He will keep on working right to the end. We are a miracle in progress.

So the next time you feel the need to see a genuine miracle, you can do one of two things. Come on over and spend a few minutes watching Kolby try to catch that mouse, or go take a look in the mirror. Your choice.

CHAPTER TWELVE:
Gimme Shelter

I will say of the Lord He is my refuge and my fortress, My God, in whom I trust.
                          - Psalm 91:2 (NIV)

C urrently in North Iowa, it's winter. Even as I write this, it is 14 degrees below zero with a wind chill of minus 55. But even that's not the worst cold I can personally remember. We had a winter back in the late 70s where we had an actual temperature of 45 below with a wind chill in excess of 100 below! Cars, if you could even get them started, would just freeze up and stop while you were driving. We had to push them to the side of the road and, in the worst cases, shoot them to put them out of their misery.

Of course we hardy Northerners laugh at such temps (did you know that "hardy" is another word for crazy?). No matter how bad the weather, you will always find somebody out in the middle of it just because we won't let any old blizzard tell us what to do (did

I mention we are stubborn, too?).

A few years ago we had a bad snow storm and my wife and I had to drive to a town about 30 miles away. It was not something we wanted to do, but we had no choice. On the way up, we saw many cars in the ditch, including one highway patrol cruiser. It's never a good sign when the cops are waiting for the tow truck. Naturally, on the way home, along a lonely stretch of back road, we slid into the ditch. Quite gracefully, I might add. We clipped the tail end of a small snow bank and lazily listed left until we plopped into a soft, deep pile of snow. When we called for a tow, the dispatcher said we had at least a four hour wait.

Right after we hung up, a man came by in a pickup. He stopped and asked if he could help. Turns out he had a four-wheel drive, but he had no chain or tow rope. As we stood there talking, another pickup came by from the opposite direction. He stopped too. He had a chain but did not have four-wheel drive. It was one of those "Jack Spratt could eat no fat; his wife could eat no lean" moments. So between the two of them we were out of the ditch in less than five minutes and on our way with a wave of the hand in thanks. And why were they out on the roads on such a day? In their own words: "To see what was up." Of course, my wife and I have an alternate version of why they stopped for us. When we left the house, we prayed for a safe trip up and back.

Through happy chance, we ended up buying a house very close to where I ended up working. Kismet, I imagine. My morning commute takes me exactly 96 seconds. I know because I timed it. On cold mornings like today or if I have to go potty (or both), I can make it in 70 seconds. But this winter, I cannot just dash home and put on my warm snuggles with Kolby in my lap and hot chocolate in my cup. This winter I am worried about Blackie.

I know that animals have their own ways of coping with bad weather and can survive in elements that would kill a human being quickly, but come on, 55 below is cold to any living creature. Several weeks ago when the temperatures were hovering in the single digits, Blackie came for supper, and I could see the little cat shivering in the cold. He alternated lifting his front paws off the frigid concrete, and his tail was wrapped tight to his body. He was thirsty, and the ice on his whiskers told me he had been trying to get water by eating snow.

I could not offer him the warmth of my home. He will let me get no closer than ten feet from him before he runs. Several times I have put Kolby in a bedroom and then tried to get Blackie to come in for just a few minutes to warm up. I hold open the door to let him feel the warmth from the kitchen. But he won't come in and afterward I just feel guilty as if I'm cheating on Kolby, like I am going behind his back to offer shelter to his mortal enemy. So I knew at this time that he would not accept my hospitality, and Kolby would not allow it. Still, I also knew I had to do something.

The next day at work I got a large heavy shipping box and put it on my work table. I found some old pieces of Styrofoam packing and appropriated those as well. My coworkers noticed me and asked what I was doing (besides wasting company time). I told them I was building Blackie a house.

They knew all about Blackie and Kolby as I had entertained (or more likely bored) them with the tales. Immediately, they became involved with the construction project, and in just a few minutes we had a group of people gathered around on company time designing a comfy house for a homeless cat.

With all the helpful suggestions, we soon had a nice warm place that any kitty would love. The sides of the box were lined with Styrofoam insulation. The floor was padded with foam rubber and covered in an old sweatshirt turned fleecy side out. For a door, we cut a hole in one side and then stapled to it a piece of t-shirt material to create a flap he could enter and leave by but would keep out the wind. To complete the house, I printed a label that said, "Blackie's Place" and attached it by the door. I figured this would keep out squirrels or any other unwanted squatters.

I took the house home at noon. I did not take it inside as I did not want Kolby to see it. It's bad enough I leave food for this interloper but to make him a house is going beyond the pale and

{ As we can see from his roofing problems,
Blackie spent more time *on* his house than he did *in* it. }

Kolby would not be happy at all. Better he simply not know.

I put the house on the kitchen landing behind the recyclable bin so it was protected from wind and snow. Now all that was left was to see if Blackie would use it.

The next day I saw Blackie approach and carefully sniff out the house, but he did not go in. He probably thought it was a trap of some kind.

I tried putting his food bowl in the house so he would have to go inside to eat. He stuck his head in but left his rear out for a quick get-away. Soon after that, I saw him sitting on top of the house. This is not what I had in mind at all when I made it.

To date, I don't know whether he uses the house or not. I've never seen him going inside or coming out, so if pressed for an opinion I would say no, he does not go in. Perhaps he has a much better hidey-hole to go to, but I doubt it. Hiding under some porch or hunkered down behind a garage cannot compare to the house I prepared.

It is all up to Blackie now. I have provided a safe place out of the wind. A place small enough that his body heat can keep him warm on the coldest nights. A place in close proximity to food and water. A place where I can keep an eye on him just in case he needs something. This is all I can do for him. He won't let me do anything more.

One of the saddest stories in the Bible is the time Jesus travelled up to the city of Jerusalem and, looking down upon it, burst into tears. He wasn't really looking at the city as it was in all its splendor. He wasn't reacting to a thriving, bustling city with people living active productive lives. He wasn't looking at that beautiful temple shining like solid gold in the sunlight. He was looking forward in time to the city as it would soon be. He saw it as a smoking ruin, overrun by Roman armies, its' people either killed or carried into captivity, and the temple thrown down until not one stone was left upon another. And He wept at that vision.

He wept because there was nothing He could do to stop it. Earlier He had lamented this fact when He said, "O Jerusalem.... How often I have wanted to gather your children together as a hen protects her chicks beneath her wings, but you wouldn't let me." Matthew 23:37 (NLT).

I was at a small zoo once. It was very small. So small that one of the exhibits was a chicken. Not exactly major zoo material but they were trying. I guess their budget consisted of chicken feed (rim shot).

The chicken was backed into the corner of her pen, and she had her wings spread out and all of her feathers puffed up. Her head darted from side to side as she watched those who were watching her. I wondered what her problem was. Then a little yellow head popped out from under one wing. It popped back in and from the other side another little yellow head peeped out cautiously. She had her whole brood under her care and was protecting them with her life if necessary.

This is the image Jesus presented. He already has protected us with His own life and now He wants to take care of us. To watch out for us. To save us from harm and danger. To provide for our needs. To gather us to Him. In His own words, He came that we might have life and have it more abundantly. Not only here on earth, but an abundant life in heaven too.

He can't do that if we won't let Him. In Ezekiel 33:11 (NIV), we see God pleading with His people, begging His children, calling them with tears, "Surely as I live, declares the Sovereign Lord, I take no pleasure in the death of the wicked, but rather that they turn from their ways and live. Turn! Turn from your evil ways! Why will you die?"

I can't keep Blackie from the cold. He won't let me. I can't give him a shelter in the time of storm. He doesn't trust me. I can't force him into the house without causing him to fear me even more than he does now and he would only try to get out as fast as he could. All I can do is provide him a safe place and hope he uses it. All I can do is be there for him. I have hopes that if he survives long enough he will learn to trust me, and we can be friends.

The other day he spoke to me for the first time. It was a small mew, but it was a communication, and that is a positive step. But I'm not sure how many more sub-zero nights he can survive. What if he is hit by a car or attacked by a dog? What if he runs into a human who decides it would be fun to hurt him? I've known people who would not think twice about taking an animal's life just because they could. I cannot protect him. He won't let me.

Jesus said, "My Father's house has many rooms." John 14:2 (NIV). Some Bible translations render this as "many mansions." Either way is OK with me. I'm not demanding when it comes to living accommodations in God's house. Believe me, I am not going to complain about the choice of wallpaper. It's going to be so much better than anything I have experienced up to this point.

I have had the pleasure of staying in a five-star hotel once in my life. It was incredible. Usually I stay in places like the motel I stayed at in Atlanta that had not one, but two bullet holes in the wall by the bed. Or there was that place in Chicago where the night clerk was grilling steaks on a hibachi right on top of the front desk.

They smelled good, but the whole thing gave me a creepy "Bates Motel" kind of vibe. I almost asked him if he was grilling one of the steaks for "Mother" but decided it was best to keep my mouth shut, lock the door to my room and get out as fast as I could in the morning. I did not take a shower.

At the five-star, there were chocolates on the pillow at night. The paper was at the door in the morning. Anything I needed was just a phone call away. Room service? You bet. Fleecy robe? Yes, please. The towels were thicker than most motel mattresses. And the best part was it was on someone else's dime. I didn't spend a cent. Now that's a life I could get used to.

Right now, Jesus is preparing a suite in the ultimate vacation destination. It's your room. Your name is on the door. It's all paid for. All you need do is make your reservation. Claim your prize. It's time to come in from the cold.

Chapter Thirteen:
The End

Can a woman forget her nursing child, or have no compassion for the child of her womb? Even these mothers may forget; but as for me, I'll never forget you!
- Isaiah 49:15 (ISV)

Well, the day that I have been dreading has finally arrived. Blackie is gone. I have not seen him in more than a week, neither has his food been eaten. It sits untouched on the kitchen landing.

For nearly a year now, Blackie has been here every day for food and water. Sometimes two or three times a day. It had gotten to the point that he would eat and leave, only to be back a few minutes later just to sit on top of his house for an hour or so. The weather and his weight have combined to collapse the roof of his house, so he has a nice dip that fits his body just right for curling up in. Kind of like a cardboard hammock. I think he sits there because he wants company. I stand and look out at him through the window, and he stares back at me. Even though there is glass between us, it passes for friendship.

There have been only a few of the coldest periods this winter when he has missed a day but usually he is here, rain or shine. That has stopped.

When he started coming over, I knew deep down that this day would be inevitable. The life span of a homeless animal is sometimes cruelly short. Lack of shelter, food, and warmth, or the inherent dangers of life on the streets combine to take their toll. As Scripture says, "The grass withers and the flowers fade." For some, they fade faster than others.

So I've been feeling a little blue today, and that took me by surprise. I really didn't even know Blackie except for the few minutes we came together around his food dish. He did not know me either. He certainly did not want to know Kolby - who would the way he acted?

We human beings are prone to forming sentimental attachments to people, places, and things. It's in our nature. How many of you have named your car? That's one area I never understood, but I'll hear people talk with great fondness about an old clunker they used to own. "Old Susie weren't much to look at but she sure got me around, consarn it." (Apparently, I only listened to grizzled old prospector types.)

Why, I've seen grown men get all misty-eyed when talking about that old Rambler they owned as a teen. Other folks I've known have let that old van sit out in the back yard for years because they could not bear the thought of junking "Old Blue" that held so many fond memories of vacation trips and school drives. So if people can get emotionally attached to an inanimate motor vehicle, you'll forgive me if I feel a little sad about losing a cat I never held or petted.

Kolby, on the other hand, was ecstatic. His actions more than anything else convinced me that Blackie was not coming back. He stopped running to the kitchen door every morning. He no longer squatted with his nose at the crack between door and jamb. He seemed lighter of heart and more playful. It was as if a heavy burden had been lifted from his shoulders. Somehow, in that prescient way that animals seem to possess, he knew.

Several mornings on my way to work I took different routes around the neighborhood to see if I could pick up any signs of Blackie (this extended my commute from 96 seconds all the way up to 163). I was looking for a small dark body lying in the road. He would be easy to spot on the snow covered streets. Several times my heart jumped when I saw in the distance a small black lump but as I got close I could see it was only dirty snow that had fallen from a passing wheel well. Of Blackie, there was no sign.

The sad part for me was that I thought we were making great progress in our relationship. We had reached the point where he would let me get within just a few feet of him without running. I would stand there and talk to him, and he would answer back. I had hoped that one day he would let me pet him but perhaps that was only wishful thinking.

I knew that I would get over my sadness. Again, that's what we humans do. We move on from painful experiences. We put them behind us and get on with our lives. That's how we survive in a world of sorrow. Our philosophy is "This too shall pass."

In the book of Revelation, we have some very special glimpses of end time events. In particular, we have a description of the redeemed as they enter into the delights of what the Scriptures term "a new heaven and a new earth." Revelation 21:4 says, "He (God) will wipe every tear from their eyes, and there will be no more death or sorrow or crying or pain. All these things are gone forever." (NLT).

That sure sounds like a happy day to me. Everything I've read about heaven makes me wish I were there right now with all my friends and family.

One thing I have always enjoyed is going to the theme parks in Florida. Universal, MGM, Disney—they are all great fun. I love the complete immersive experience. Once you walk through the gates you are in a different world. For a day, nothing exists outside of the world they have created for you. No worries, no troubles, no cares. Just fun. But as far as I can remember, I've never cried when I entered one of those parks. I shed no tears when I step on the cobblestones of Main Street USA. Goofy does not have to hand me a tissue to wipe my eyes. I'm there for a good time. I'm not sad when I hit the Haunted House attraction for a third or fourth time.

Why, then, are there tears in the eyes of the redeemed? The answer is both simple and painful. We will be missing some of our friends and family who are not there with us. As my sister-in-law has maintained since she was a chubby-cheeked cherub, a vacation is not a vacation without the "whole family."

We will cry tears of joy as we gather with friends and family who are there and tears of sorrow when we see who among our loved ones have chosen not to be there.

Let me be as clear as I can on this point because the Bible itself is clear as crystal: not all shall be there. Only those who have "washed their robes" in the blood of Jesus will walk the streets of gold. If you do not believe me, I invite you to get out your Bible and study the topic. Read the plain statements of Jesus Christ and the stern warnings He has for those who refuse His invitation. Here, let me save you the time. Here's the words of Jesus Himself on the issue: "Not everyone who says to me, 'Lord, Lord,' will enter the kingdom of heaven, but only the one who does the will of my Father who is in heaven." Matthew 7: 21 (NIV).

There will be tears, and then we will move on. We will heal as time passes. The Scriptures tells us, "See, I will create new heavens and a new earth. The former things will not be remembered, nor will they come to mind." Isaiah 65: 17 (NIV).

We always focus on our part of the final events and how it will impact mankind, but how about God's feelings in all this. How does it affect Him? The Bible calls God's final destruction of the wicked His "strange act." Isaiah 28: 21 (KJV). This is not something He is comfortable with. It is not something He is looking forward to. Just as a parent does not enjoy the punishment of a child, God does not enjoy this, His final act, in the plan of salvation.

146

While we will forget and move on, God has a long memory. Will He ever forget the lost? If we think that we knew our friends and family well, God knew them on a level we could never reach. He knew them personally—each and every one. He knew them before they were born. He knew every atom and every molecule that made up their being. He knew their every care and every fear, every laugh and every sigh. And He loved them as we could never love. He will miss them.

Some commentators have speculated that the only reminder of the terrible consequences of sin will be the marks of the crucifixion on the body of Jesus. These scars will forever serve as a reminder of the high price God paid to ransom you and me.

Personally, I believe there will be other scars God carries too. Scars that we cannot see; scars that run deep beneath the surface. Emotional scars over the ones He could not save, the ones He drew with cords of love, but they would not respond. I believe these scars will never fully heal.

Kolby moved on very fast from Blackie. It will take me a little longer. God will miss the lost for all eternity. It's part of what makes Him God.

 Epilogue

It was a Saturday night just around twilight, the time when the sun has finished its shift for the day but the moon is still at the time clock punching in. Things are visible only as shapes and shadows in the dusk. I stood at the refrigerator holding the door wide open trying to find something to eat.

When I did that as a kid, my father would yell, "Shut the door! You're letting all the cold air out! Whatta ya' born in a barn?" When my great nephews and nieces do it now, I shout, "Shut the door! You're letting all the cold air out! Whatta ya' born in a barn?" Such is the great circle of life.

Since I am all grown up now and my father is no longer there to shout at me, I can leave the fridge door open all night if I want to (I did that by accident one night. Needless to say, there was warm milk for breakfast. Bleh!).

Of course, the fridge was filled with all kinds of things to eat. I just didn't want any of that stuff. It was all too familiar to me, and I was now trying to decide if I had enough gumption left to get in the car and bring home a ginormous burrito from the Ginormous Burrito Restaurant just down the street. I am not exaggerating (much) when I say that these things are as big as a pillow. They are very handy for late night snacking as you don't even have to get out of bed, just flip over and start to gnaw.

Suddenly, Kolby shot past me to the kitchen door.

He stuck his nose on the door jamb and drew in a deep breath. His tail began to twitch. No. It couldn't be. Kolby looked up at me and meowed loudly.

With a sudden rush of anticipation, I stepped to the door and pulled back the curtain. Out on the sidewalk, something small and dark was moving toward the house. It looked like an animal of some kind but without light I could not tell what it was. A few feet closer and it would activate the motion sensor and turn on the outside light.

Just then, the sensor tripped and light bathed the landing and steps. There stood a small jet black cat with deep emerald green eyes.

"Blackie!" I shouted. "Where have you been?"

Hearing my loud shout, Blackie sat down and looked up at the windows to see my smiling face staring stupidly out at him. He meowed softly.

"Wait right there," I told him, "I'll get your supper."

Turning to Kolby, I said excitedly, "Blackie's back, kitty! What do you think about that?"

Kolby stared up at me with a look of resignation: *"Aw nuts. Here we go again."*

KEEP UP WITH KOLBY

My Adventures With Kolby
Charles Caponi

When Chuck adopted a cat from his local Humane Society, he never realized how life-altering his decision would be. Read about his many adventures in pet ownership in this hilarious little book, *My Adventures with Kolby (and I Don't Mean the Cheese)*. A portion of the proceeds from sales of this book go to help other animals find loving homes and owners they can drive crazy too.

Kolby and the Really Bad Dream
Chuck Caponi & Matthew J Lucio

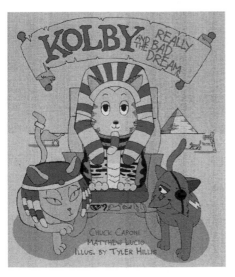

Kolby's first picture book for kids! Join Kolby as he journeys back to ancient Egypt and the good ole days when adults used to worship cats...and then see why this is just a completely awful idea as it backfires on Kolby. Kids will enjoy the rich, colorful illustrations (and finding the secret jokes hidden throughout)

Ages 3 & up!

Follow Kolby on Facebook! Why? Because the internet makes it possible to get regular updates from the life of a cat. That's how you know you've made it in life. Plus, you'll get to hear Kolby stories before they make it into the next book!

facebook.com/kolbycat

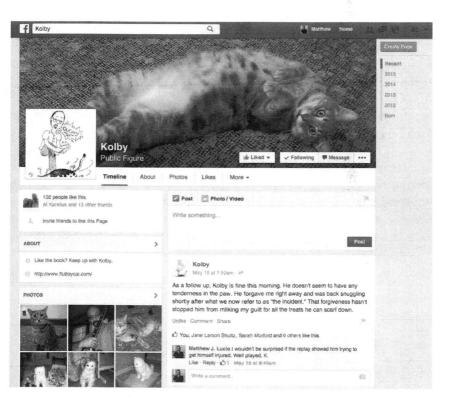

Shadows and Scars || T. Jason Vanderlaan

"We wander through life, searching for belonging and validation. Here in this valley, we are pursued by the shadows of our regrets and haunted by the scars of our past. We are lost, but in seeking, we will find, and in finding, we will be found."

Shadows & Scars is a messy book. Through poetry, T. Jason Vanderlaan tells a story, but not one that begins in the beginning, or ends at the end. This is about being in the middle, about wandering. This is about loose ends and unresolved issues and the tension of living in the in-between. All the while, dreams of peace and rest float just out of reach – elusive invitations, like fireflies dancing in the summer night.

Within the framework of searching for belonging and validation, Vanderlaan explores a variety of topics – growing up in a divorced family, falling in love, giving and receiving broken hearts, losing the way and finding regret, the ache of letting go, wrestling with forgiveness and hope and trust. When the dust settles, these frayed ends of family, romance, and spirituality tangle together. The result is in an incomplete yet beautiful display, a portrait of the fearful desire to know and be known, to love and be loved, to seek and find and be found.

End || Matthew J. Lucio

Join author Matthew J. Lucio on a imaginative, 31-part devotional journey through the Book of Revelation. Though many see Revelation as a dark, confusing tale that seems out of place in the Bible, Lucio focuses on Revelation as a playground for the spiritual imagination. Far from surrendering to confusion over Revelation's army of deep symbology, Lucio suggests that that Christians need a brave, fresh look at the practical lessons Revelation has for us today. While *End* doesn't promise to solve all of Revelation's riddles, it will help you appreciate the good news it contains.

God'shadow || Daniel de Sevén

Daniel de Sevén takes us on a journey deeper into doubt through a variety of short, creative essays meant to recall dormant doubts in the reader or else to create new ones. For many it will be an uncomfortable adventure, but it is, the author argues, a necessary one because doubt is the delivery room of faith.

But be warned: this book isn't about the author trying to inductively prove a point. Rather, it is at once disjointed and communal, allowing readers to join the discussion and reach their own conclusions - which the author feels is the only kind of conclusions worth reaching. This isnt teaching; this is discovering.

Kolby's special friends:

Judy Grantham
Jack and Jaunice Bull
Terry and Nancy Eldridge
Adelaide Delano
William and Louise Smith
Janet Cleveland
Mary and Mike Rivers
Lee and Yvonne Weber
Dan Pease and Bettie Swarts
Shawn and Toleka King
Kim Caponi

Kolby would like to apologize if he missed anyone. He feels bad if he left anyone out (Editor's note: no he doesn't. He thinks only of himself).

Made in the USA
Middletown, DE
28 June 2015